WELL YOU NEEDN'T

Well You Needn't

Joel Lewis

MY LIFE AS A JAZZ FAN

Hanging Loose Press | Brooklyn, New York

Published by Hanging Loose Press, PO Box 150608, Brooklyn, NY11215.

www.hangingloosepress.com
Printed in the United States of America 10 9 8 7 6 5 4 3 2 1

Design: Aimee Harrison
Author Photo: Sandy Flitterman-Lewis

Cover Art: Norman Lewis (1909–1979), *Untitled*, 1948, oil on canvas,
49 7/8 x 41 5/8 inches / 126.7 x 105.7 cm, signed;
private collection; © Estate of Norman Lewis;
Courtesy of Michael Rosenfeld Gallery LLC, New York, NY

OTHER BOOKS BY JOEL LEWIS

Tosses As It Is Untroubled, 1979 (Gaede's Pond Press)
Japan In a Dishpan, 1979 (Gaede's Pond Press)
Bullets in the Potato Salad, 1980 (Gaede's Pond Press)
Three Works, 1983 (Gaede's Pond Press)
Entropia, 1986 (Gaede's Pond Press)
House Rent Boogie, 1992 (Yellow Press)
Palookas of the Ozone 1992 (e.g. press)
North Jersey Gutter Helmet, 1995 (Oasis Press)
Vertical's Currency: New and Selected Poems, 1999 (Talisman House)
The Tasks of the Youth Leagues, 2005 (Oasis Press)
Learning From New Jersey, 2007 (Talisman House)
Surrender When Leaving Coach, 2012 (Hanging Loose Press)
North River Rundown, 2012 (Accent Editions)
My Shaolin: A Poem of Staten Island, 2016 (Hanging Loose Press)

EDITED

Bluestones and Salt Hay: An Anthology of Contemporary New Jersey Poets, 1990 (Rutgers University Press)
On The Level Everydays: Selected Talks of Ted Berrigan, 1997 (Talisman House)
Reality Prime: Selected Poems of Walter Lowenfels, 1998 (Talisman House)

ISBN: 978-1-934909-80-5

In Memory of

Steve Dalachinsky

Michael Gizzi

Bob Porter

"No matter how you feel, get up, dress up and show up."

—SONNY ROLLINS

"Sans le jazz, la vie serait une erreur"
(Without jazz, life would be a mistake)

—BORIS VIAN

"Improvisation=dreams minus meaning."

—from *The Lost Book of Bop*: *The Intensity of Relations*

Contents

ARCHIE SHEPP RECALLS HIS FIRST ENCOUNTER WITH MILES DAVIS

"I allowed myself to be
talked into it and so
I approached Miles Davis
very delicately, because he
was mobbed
by a coterie of admirers
and was deep in conversation
with one of them.

I dared to interrupt
by saying, 'Mr. Davis,
my name is Archie Shepp.'

He said: 'Archie who?' I
said: 'Archie Shepp.' He
said: 'FUCK YOU!'

I was a young man but
I had two children and
I was married.
I had respected him
but felt that he was
totally disrespectful of me. So,
I responded in kind:
'Fuck you
—who the FUCK are you!'

We got into this
terrible argument.
One of his sons was there

and he was a boxer, so Miles
says to me,
'My son will KICK your ASS!' And
I said to him:
'I'll kick your ass on the bandstand,
that's where the music is made.'

At that point, he took another
attitude altogether. It was rather like
the Old West. He rasped: 'Take
your horn out,
MOTHERFUCKER!'

So that's how
I got to sit in
with Miles Davis."

(opposite) Dennis Stock, "Bill Crow, New York City, 1958."
From Stock's book, *Jazz Street.* Courtesy of Magnum Photo.

HOTEL
SAFETY ZONE
NO PARKING

FIRST VERSE

MY LIFE AS A JAZZ FAN

BOOK ONE

How did one become a jazz fan in the 1970s? As a teenager growing up in Northern New Jersey, jazz was something you associated with the corny sounds that one's parents and their cronies enjoyed. Jazz was still in the air, but it was mostly associated with World War Two nostalgia and the aging big bands that would still make appearances on the Ed Sullivan show or at the Hollywood Palace. I still remember the cringe-inducing TV appearance of Count Basie's band playing a Beatles melody with all the enthusiasm of deserters facing a firing squad. In my sullen preteen years, Louis Armstrong's Beatlemania-era hit, "Hello, Dolly," was de rigueur at every wedding and bar mitzvah I attended. The message was very clear: rock music was NOW! as well as being a subversive music that baffled adults.

To roll things back: I grew up as a fat, unhappy kid, with tendencies towards isolating behavior, in a town on the Hudson Palisades opposite midtown Manhattan. It was a safe and fairly placid working-class town, but I had hardly any friends in the neighborhood—I went to the Yeshiva of Hudson County, a Jewish day school, where the kids I was friends with lived, bus rides away in a nearby city. I spent my off hours and weekends reading comic books and *Mad Magazine* or walking along Boulevard East, watching the tugs push the railroad car floats across the Hudson. Sometimes I would play Chinese handball by myself, accompanied by my transistor radio blaring a Yankees game.

Summer brought some respite from this tedium, when we loaded up the car and drove to the Catskills, where I'd spend the summer hanging out with a gang of kids—many of whom were classmates at my day school. But then the bankruptcy of my father's embroidery factory put an end to such summer idylls.

My father, a survivor of the Auschwitz-Birkenau labor camps (one of his non-remunerated jobs was mining coal without benefit of a helmet), was part of a group of Holocaust survivors who settled in our area and became involved in what they called "the embroidery business," an industry centered in the North Hudson communities where we all lived. The embroidered patterns that found their way onto wedding gowns and brassieres were produced by heavy machines originally brought to the area by Swiss and German immigrants in the late 19th century; then successive immigrant communities worked in the small, mostly one- or two-machine shops that seemed to have slipped between the one- and two-family homes that made up our community.

After a few years of working with a partner, my father had decided to strike out on his own. The garment business was still strong in Manhattan in the late '50s, before the rise of the cheaper Asian markets. His one-machine shop was named after his hometown in Poland, *Koval Embroidery,* and was located on Harrison Place in West New York. My mother (who was raised in Brooklyn) did the books; my father hired a "watcher"—simply someone who kept an eye on the working machine as well as repairing threads breaks on the fly. (Nomenclature was not a priority in this sector of the *shmatte* business). My dad's seamstress was the wife of a local cop—which came in handy when he needed to run the machine on a Sunday, against local ordinance. Everyone else's father had some sort of embroidery-related business, ranging from selling supplies to "jobbing" out assignments from the Garment District textile firms for the gritty work of manufacturing the trimming that would eventually be affixed to women's garments.

My father's business reversal marked our entire family as a failure. He got caught in the Kennedy-era recession and had to declare bankruptcy. My parents cashed in the savings bonds that family members had given us when I was born to buy food, and my father took a mysterious trip to Montreal to borrow money from a friend of his from "the camps." Then he ended up working for his former business partner. It was not until I became an adult that I realized the impact that it must have had on him. It was the sort of situation in which some men "go out for a pack of cigarettes" and never come back to their family, while other men would understand the desperation of such decisions.

Coinciding with my family's slide down the monkey bars of capitalism was the emergence of the Beatles. It almost seemed like all of us in the Yeshiva schoolyard were possessed by British dybbuks. One day, we were just eight-year-olds playing Frozen Tag, then the Beatles appeared on Ed Sullivan and, by the next morning, we were all yammering about Liverpool and the River Mersey and growing our hair long. Soon, we were collecting

Beatle 45s as well as Beatle trading cards. We spoke Carnaby Street slang like "fab," "gear," "birds," "boss" and, after a long day at Yeshiva, we would proclaim, "I'm fagged out!" Sandy Alter, a *shammes's* son, suddenly started speaking in a Liverpudlian accent to match the collarless Edwardian jacket he began wearing to school every day. And we all shared an enduring belief that Ringo was Jewish: after all, he had a big Jewish-type nose, as well as having changed his name (as so many Jewish families had done) from Richard Starkey to Ringo Starr. Indeed, my family had gone from Leyzzki (my birth surname) to Lewis. I sometimes thought we should change our names again and go someplace where our friends didn't look down on us as *losers.*

All of us *Yeshiva bochers* were possessed by the Limey *kinehora.* After burning out too many nine-volt batteries on my father's Westclox radio, I began saving up my allowance, cashing in soda bottles and hanging on to every quarter any relative gave me in order to get my own six-transistor radio.

But while everyone else seemed to be a Beatles fan (jeez, my mom thought Paul was cute!), my band was the Rolling Stones. What was it about the Stones that appealed to me as a grade schooler? I knew nothing about their deep roots in American blues, rhythm and blues, and rock and roll. Their leering sexual innuendos sailed over my head and, frankly, they really were not aiming their music at my demographic—the band's original fan base was students at the University of London, who admired their early set lists consisting of nothing but obscure black American music.

I think their outsider status appealed to me. Unlike the other British bands that donned matching band outfits and worked very hard at appealing to both young girls and their mums, the Stones showed up on national TV in a motley array of sweatshirts, denim jackets and Teddy Boy cast-offs (save for their immaculately dressed drummer Charlie Watts). There were no Rolling Stones comic books, Rolling Stones bubble gum cards or a Rolling Stones movie (and when Jagger & Co. took a stab at celluloid, they sure weren't going to do another *Hard Day's Night*—they first tried to acquire the rights to *A Clockwork Orange,* but were outbid by Stanley Kubrick).

It never occurred to me to learn an instrument. Simply, I knew my parents really couldn't afford to pay for lessons, and I had enough self-awareness to realize how undisciplined I was. It was also hard to imagine myself, even in my daydreams, on stage performing without getting laughed at.

"WASN'T BORN TO FOLLOW"

A soft dream about the Brill Building circa
'62, Kong-sized smoke rings still spilling off
the Times Square lightscape.

Don Kirchner approaches me: "Who the fuck are you?" I
freeze. He then asks: "But are you . . . Jew-ish?"
I nod while showing him the botch-job on my schlong.

"I guess you'll do," the future Monkee Svengali mutters and
soon I find myself in a cubicled room with
Neil Sedaka, Carole King, Barry Mann, Cynthia Weil and others.

Doc Pomus enters and runs over my feet with
his wheelchair: "AND WHO THE FUCK ARE YOU!" he bellows
& then an abrupt "Get busy! And write some HITS!"

I get down to work but can only come up with
"America Was Founded in a Drizzle" which I think
Jay and the Americans might like.

Ellie Greenwich and Jeff Barry straighten me out by kicking
my ass, shouting, "You got the melancholy and the
sadness, but not much else!"   "Wait," I shout

knocking over my papaya drink, "this tune would
be great for Little Eva: "My Mouth
Is the Lips of Your Mother Before You Were Born."

Kirchner joins Greenwich and Barry in stomping me. I don't mind
as I realize I'm dreaming and while I'm being tossed out onto Broadway
"Old Men Have Syntactic Minds" flashes inside me—

A new dreamland hit for the Righteous Brothers! Suddenly
Neil Diamond pulls me out of the gutter & slips me a fin.
He's dressed like Yussel Rabinovitch from his take on *The Jazz Singer*.

"Get yourself cleaned up, you *putz*," he snarls and behind him is
Sir Laurence Olivier, dressed like Yussel's Cantor-dad, anguished,
rending his garments, bellowing: "I HEF NO SON!"

SECOND VERSE

MY LIFE AS A JAZZ FAN
BOOK TWO

My musical lifepath changed one spring night in 1970. Like most New York City area teenage intellectuals, my favorite radio station was WNEW-FM, a classic "freeform" station, playing cutting-edge rock, with each show reflecting the D.J.'s taste. Jonathan Schwartz was the thinking girl's heart throb famed both for reading his short stories on the air and for his thematic programming that might, for example, start a block with "The Rain, The Park and Other Things," and after three more rain songs, ending with "Here Comes the Sun."

Like many other young male listeners, I developed a crush on Allison Steele, "The Nightbird," the station's sultry-voiced overnight D.J. She began her show with flutes and poetry, and always managed to sound as if she was addressing you personally, like some sort of auditory hallucination. I was so taken with her that I'd call up the show—and she'd actually talk to me!

At some point, she recognized my voice, and the sultry tones gave way to the hard-knocks voice of a woman who had been in radio since the late '40s. As to my then ambitions of being a D.J.? "Kid, you gotta watch yourself. There are a lot of assholes out there." Now, as I grow into my dotage, I realize that the Night Bird's adage was less a specific warning than it was a universal truism.

Rosko was the station's only black D.J. He was also the most disinterested in his tone and delivery—he seemed to suggest that he was doing YOU, the listener, a favor just by bothering to show up. Rosko specialized in playing the black rock of the Chambers Brothers, Sly and the Family Stone, Taj Majal, Love, and Jimi Hendrix—those spiritual grandpas of Prince—as well as poetry or to read a long critique of the still-raging Vietnam War, both accompanied by ethnic chants courtesy of a Nonesuch *World Explorer* LP.

"Miles Davis . . . "Spanish Key"" growled Rosko on one fortuitous evening and then came 16 minutes of unprecedented sound: instrumental, and with a trumpet as lead instrument. Unlike the progressive rock I loved, "Spanish Key" did not resolve melodically, nor even seem to have an identifiable melody. The listener was forced to accept the performer's sound world on its own terms. Who was this Miles Davis, anyway? I got my answer the next day at Communications, a hippie-run record-cum-head shop that only stocked albums that you heard on WNEW. I once recall the hippie-dude proprietor yelling with zeal at some hapless square who had wandered in, "You want the Carpenters? THE CARPENTERS!! Get the fuck out of my store!"

"Spanish Key" was on the *Bitches Brew* album. I bought it (two discs for the price of one sealed the deal for me). "Hey, that platter's Hip!" Mr. Hippie Dude declared as he gave me my change. At home, I found myself transfixed by Abdul Mati Klarwein's wrap-around artwork. His LSD-drenched landscapes would later be draped all over Santana's *Abraxas.* What's going on here, I thought, especially this Miles Davis, a guy as old as my father; and these liner notes (all in lower case) by Ralph J. Gleason (I knew him only as a *Rolling Stone* editor). He was treating this unknown as if he was Clapton or Hendrix. Over the next few weeks, I played the album nearly every evening. This is not to say that I "got it," but I was intrigued enough to investigate further. Over the course of my high school years, I became a full-fledged jazz fan.

In my peer group, though, no one seemed even vaguely interested except the drummers who were under the spell of Buddy Rich. Ah, loud-mouthed, talent-wasting Buddy! Employing a pencil to tap out paradiddles on Johnny Carson's desk! Suggesting that the Cream's drummer Ginger Baker's ass "should be stuffed in a rocket and shot into outer space!" The beads, the Nehru jackets, his obsessive hatred of Billy Cobham. Those drummer boys loaned me his albums—each one left me more depressed than the one before. Most of it seemed to be some old guy trying to stay hip with his swinging versions of "Jesus Christ, Superstar."

WRVR, the radio station of Riverside Church, was the only full-time jazz station in New York City. My jazz horizons expanded as I began listening to it. I was led to a lifelong passion for tenor sax master John Coltrane. Today he is on a postage stamp; he's been depicted in a Memorex TV ad; and he's acknowledged as an important figure in the pantheon of Hip-Hop forefathers. But back in the early '70s he was unknown outside of the jazz world. My first "Trane" purchase was the Impulse album simply called *Coltrane,* with a bluish, abstract photo of him on the cover. I would play "Out of This World" over and over again, much to the consternation of my parents: ironically, they found Coltrane's saxophone sound far more objectionable than the squalling rock guitarists I used to play on our crummy Magnavox stereo.

Unknown to my parents, I would frequently take my fifteen-year-old self on a bus into scary Manhattan to visit the midtown record shops. My limited means favored the King Karol Sales Annex on 10th Avenue and 42nd Street, a large store brimming with $1.99 "cut-outs," the deeply discounted or remaindered bargains that the place featured. I acquired, quite cheaply, most of Frank Zappa's output on the Verve label, and I began building the basics of my own jazz collection. Occasionally, I'd go over to their main store east on 42nd, near 6th Avenue. At the time, Karol's could make good on their boast that they kept every in-print U.S. LP in stock. Sadly, though, I couldn't afford their prices. But I did make friends with a record clerk named Ric Colbeck, a relatively unknown British jazz trumpet player. Years later, his reputation was rescued from absolute obscurity: Thurston Moore of the band Sonic Youth put Colbeck's Fontana album, *The Sun Is Coming Up*, on his list of top ten great "free jazz" classics. Colbeck was also part of Noah Howard's quartet, as demonstrated on an ESP-Disk—the record label that was the primary documenter of the early New York City avant-garde community.

As a young jazz tyro, I was amazed—I could chat with a real live jazz musician. And for Ric I was an audience, a receptive one for his tales of trying to make it in the New York City music scene. Ric told me how Miles Davis stole the idea of the electric trumpet from him, how hard it was to survive as a white European among the Black avant-garde scene, and darkly muttered about "heavy scenes in the Bronx." I didn't really care what he told me, as he seemed to take me seriously. No one really knows what happened to Colbeck, other than that he is no longer alive. And only recently did I learn that in his early days as an artist, Archie Rand, a marvelous painter and fellow jazz fan, actually worked alongside Colbeck at a downtown record shop.

BIX

Born too early in Davenport, Iowa
Old School Teutonic Parents
Bad Teeth/Poor Student
The "young man with a horn" syndrome.
Nights inside the drunk submarine.

Legend Wolverine band played
a '20s version of Punk.
Mostly frat smokers and gym dances,
though "In A Mist" put him ahead
of the harmonic game.

Eight bars of solo cornet played
in a snappy tux but stuck
inside the belly of Paul Whiteman's
mammoth fake-jazz orchestra
"Like towing the Lusitania through a sea of Mars bars."
The Whiteman band is the Pink Floyd of the era
Bix's solos are sad zephyrs against
the forehead of nightly numbing arrangements.

His stern parents in
the plush velvet seats
of their local bijou:
"That's our Leon!"—Bix
in a newsreel, next to buddy "Tram,"
stone drunk and smirking.

"MIDRIFF"

He gave
  up
on the progress
  of jazz
after 1935
  which marks
the point
  when
electronic
  microphones
became
  commonplace
in studios
  thus
destroying
  the fragile line
between
  the listener
& the soloist
  facing
the black center
  of the inscribing
horn.

FLIP TOP

Facebook friend Ted Curson
died last night.

Age 77, a Montclair resident
who earned his jazz stripes
in an early Mingus band. His
trumpet on the frontline next to
Eric Dolphy's arcana
of wood and brass.

Met him in '02 at Hoboken's
now ghost Barnes & Noble as
he read *The Economist*
in an obsidian leather trench coat.

"I made tons more money playing
six months in a Mingus tribute band
than in the three years
I played with Charles!"

And of his absence from the American scene?
"I'm huge in Finland! Get on a Helsinki tram
& you'll see ads with me selling milk
for the Sata Maito dairy."

And here?

"I'm just sitting with a latte
waiting for my wife."

BOOKER ERVIN IN EUROPEAN EXILE (1965)

Oh man, now it's 2 a.m. with the fringe moonlight
on the Jai Alai fronton.
The shifting forms going
off in a sleep-short brain.

"Where?" The Beatles & their kin
are Panzering jazz
stateside & here it is . . . *where?*
Baden-Baden? Danzig? Milano?
And I can't help myself
but I'm kinda attached to those stingy-brims and
same ol' horn rims worn cover after cover,
Savoy to Prestige to Blue Note.

It's a culture burden, you know?
"Want some sandwiches, Book?"
There's no aristocracy on the bandstand and
tomorrow it will be
yet another bombed-out and now rebuilt
anonymous West German city.

That snow globe behind the register?
Danke, I'd like that one for my littlest girl.

THE COMPLETE HOT FIVE AND HOT SEVEN RECORDINGS

Deeply pissed off
by Little Rock Central High School's
fierce desegregation battle

Louis Armstrong
slammed President Eisenhower as
"GUTLESS!"

& declared Governor Faubus
to be nothing more than a
"NO-GOOD MOTHERFUCKER!"

The latter appellation
(for newspaper consumption)
rendered into "Uneducated Plowboy"

"MINOR MEETING"
SONNY CLARK, PIANIST

Who remains among your running
buddies? Paul Chambers:
a forgotten ghost. The aptly named
Shadow Wilson. Intimations
of Ernie Henry.

The '50s couldn't have been that
great for you and your pals.
And the detached gestures
of television formed the word "corny"
with your lips. While this nation lost sleep
over Red spies, you were a reluctant
card-carrying apparatchik of the junk brigade
and a grandmaster of hard bop's topiary maze.

THE INCREDIBLE JIMMY SMITH

. . . gave the term "woodshedding" a bright
new precision when he vanished for a year
into a Philadelphia warehouse
with a loaner Hammond organ.

His discipline and assiduous practice
helped wipe away that instrument's
often joke image with
electrified renderings
of bebop.

Blue Note's Alfred Lion
heard Smith perform
one bitter February night
in a Harlem club.
And so stunned
by what he heard,
signed him to the label
after the last set.
It was 1956.

In the following two years,
Smith recorded and released
13 albums. The sound of his Model B-3
became part of the masculine discourse
heard on the bar and grill circuit
until the arrival of disco.

But "The Sermon" lives on
and "grits 'n' gravy music" was

not just a promo man's too clever
colonnade: it was the obvious
code for Smith's electronic stride
and the democracy vested
inside the old feelings.

BRIDGE

MY LIFE AS A JAZZ FAN

BOOK THREE

Having spent all my money and brain power on collecting jazz albums, and so being wholly unprepared financially or grade-wise for college, I ended up at William Paterson College, located just outside of nearby Paterson. To my amazement, they had a jazz program; I signed up immediately for a jazz history course with trumpeter and composer Thad Jones. This was 1973; Thad was beloved by both boppers and big band enthusiasts for the jazz orchestra he co-led with drummer Mel Lewis. And in the racial confusion of the post-Civil Rights era, the band got much play, as its leaders were a black guy from Detroit and a Jewish drummer (né Sokoloff) who had paid his dues behind the drum kit with three years in the ultra-white Stan Kenton Orchestra.

Beyond his skills as an arranger and bandleader, Thad was a great composer whose "A Child is Born" remains a standard today. His arranging and composing skills overshadowed his abilities as a performer, although his trumpet playing brought praise from the likes of Thelonius Monk, Charles Mingus, and Miles Davis, who once declared, "I'd rather hear Thad Jones miss a note than hear Freddie Hubbard make ten!"

Whatever his other skills, pedagogy was not Thad's strong suit—though perhaps that assessment is hasty, since he didn't show up to teach very much anyway. His classes were most often covered by Vinson Hill, a pianist and pioneer jazz educator who took his teaching seriously, and later joined the faculty as an assistant professor. Thad, on the other hand, mostly played LPs from his record collection and uttered such cryptic non-sequiturs as: "Does the name Tricky Sam Nanton mean anything to you?" or "When I was a young cat, when we said that someone was funky, it meant that cat smelled!" No matter, for me it was a thrill to be in his presence—even if Thad gave me the hipster version of a stink-eye when I'd bring up my avant-garde trumpet faves like Don Cherry. And when, a few years later, Thad was awarded an honorary doctorate from Willie Pee, he didn't give no boring speech. He reached under his robes, pulled out a trumpet and played it! It was the hippest graduation ceremony in 1977 America.

In the spring of my freshman year, I was walking along Bergenline Avenue in North Bergen on a sunny April day, when I saw a shop across from Delancy's candy store that seemed to have sprung out of nowhere. It was called Jazz, Etc. and the big sign in the window read, "Everything from Bunk to Monk." It seemed like a blunt and forceful message from a higher power. I crossed the street and peered inside. "Holy crap! It's a jazz record shop!" Venturing in, I heard Dizzy Gillespie pouring out of the speakers. The walls were plastered with LP covers: Charlie Ventura, Alan Eager, Sonny Criss, and other great but relatively obscure figures so beloved by the serious fan.

The shop owner was Bob Porter, recently canned from his gig at Prestige Records in Bergenfield, a few miles up the road when it was acquired by Fantasy Records. That label could afford to expand because they'd made millions with Creedence Clearwater Revival. Bob would later gain fame as a host on Newark's jazz station WBGO as well as his long-running NPR show "Portraits in Blue." And, true to the code of every indie book, comic book, and record shop guy, he was taciturn and aloof. His assistant Eddie was a young cat from Brooklyn who played tenor and was studying with the great blind pianist Lennie Tristano. Over the long course of time that I hung out there, I would frequently find Eddie walking around the store with his eyes closed, bumping into the bins ("I was just trying to see what Lennie's world was like"), singing Charlie Parker solos, playing Diana Ross albums ("Lennie says she's the new Billie Holiday"), and reading the selected writings of Leon Trotsky ("Lennie is into him, so I decided to check him out!"). Poor Eddie also spent most of his paltry pay on psychoanalysis, because Lennie had told him, "Eddie, you got to resolve your issues with your father if you want to be a great player."

A few months after my introduction to Jazz, Etc., Bob called me at home. "Hey Joel, Eddie split. You want the gig?" And so on Lincoln's birthday, 1975, I handed my cashier's apron back to my employers at the Pantry Pride supermarket, and began my career in Jazzland. In making the transition from customer to flunky, I realized two things—one: Bob was REALLY politically conservative, and two: he HATED the avant-garde jazz that I was enamored with. Although I was in my high radical phase at college—Karl Marx my toilet reading, "Justice for the Rosenbergs" rallies, and being able to spell "bourgeoisie" without recourse to a dictionary—political discussions were easy enough to sidestep. Albert Ayler was another matter. Bob: ("Joel, turn that shit off!") Cecil Taylor ("that guy is jiving you"); and Gato Barbieri in his avant-garde phase ("Joel, turn that shit off, man, that guy can't play and did somebody drive a nail into his foot while he was recording??!!").

Bob's great love was bop and the soul jazz that, at that time, appalled me. He had produced much of Prestige's soul catalog and had had a hit with Charles Earland's version of "More Today Than Yesterday." The background music in the store was mostly the albums he had produced. I found these pretty indistinguishable from one another, with each organ group kind of morphing into the next. Work, such as it was, consisted of filling and shipping records through the mail-order catalog that was the heart of the business. The big sellers were the collector's labels that mostly consisted of airchecks (recordings of radio broadcasts) that audiophile jazz nuts had recorded in the '50s when tape recorders were first introduced.

The king of such aircheck enterprises was the mysterious Boris Rose, an engineer for the Mutual Broadcast System back then who'd had access to the best equipment. Issuing air checks without permission was illegal and since Rose was somewhat paranoid (if also witty and mischievous), his LP sleeves were rudimentary, with carefully obfuscated details. Terrified, for example, that song publishers would have him arrested, he would change a song's title as it was listed on the sleeve. "My Favorite Things" became "Stuff I'm Partial To," and "Embraceable You" was "You So Good to Hug." He also had a perverse streak, given to issuing, say, Woody Herman's *Second Herd Volume 2* without bothering to put out a Volume One. And—to the delight of my kid brother—Boris even brought out a bootleg of the legendary *Grand Crepitation (farting) Contest* album.

The shop's Big Day was Saturday, when the "jazz beaus" from New York would venture across the Hudson to hang out and peruse our bins. There was Jerry Valburn, who was in possession of literally more than a million feet of Duke Ellington airchecks on tape, (eventually purchased by the Smithsonian). A lot of our customers were, like Artie Zimmerman of Zim Records, for instance, proprietors of small labels that specialized in reissuing out-of-print LPs, as well as airchecks and club recordings. Bob had his own Phoenix label, one of the few that bothered to pay something to the featured artist's heirs.

Then there were the hardcore collectors obsessed with Prestige "yellow labels," that is, Prestige records of a certain vintage when the LP labels were the shade of old Velveeta. No Saturday would be complete without a call from the late Harvey Pekar, fondly remembered for his *American Splendor* comics, but then just a pain in the ass from Cleveland. Harvey would always phone in wanting to discuss Gene "Jug" Ammons records with Jug's ex-producer Bob. (Bob would growl, "Tell that nut I'm out of town!")

And, or course, among the myriad bald pates, goatees, and bad postures, rarely did the female form pay us a visit. The only women jazz fans seemed to be the wives of the most severely demented guys, and I suppose they became fans just to understand what the fuck their husbands were talking about and wasting their money on. When an attractive woman popped in to buy a disk—even if it was some commercial crap like George Benson or Grover Washington—it was an event we'd discuss for days.

Listening to these men, I got a total anecdotal history of jazz. Guys who hung with Bird, found Red Rodney a dentist for his bad teeth, watched Woody Herman pee on the leg of a semi-comatose Serge Chaloff, drove Duke Jodan back from a gig and then watched documentaries on soybean harvesting with him on woeful early AM TV. I was the "kid" and that rare kid who liked jazz, as their own kids were all rock fans—I was even forgiven for my peculiar taste for free-form sonic blowouts. In retrospect, Archie Shepp howling away was my version of Metallica, an angry music that soothed my unhappy college self with dreams of social revolution and/or a girlfriend.

The most memorable of these characters was Teddy Reig, the man who produced Charles Parker for Savoy and whose huge frame kept Bird's casket from sliding into the rainy streets of Harlem after the funeral at the Abyssinian Baptist Church. He was genuine jazz history, managing Count Basie's band, going out and scoring junk for his musicians so they could complete sessions—Teddy was on a first name basis with the various gangsters who provided fuel for the jazz life. Teddy would barrel into our store, still fragrant from the garlicky knoblewurst sausage he had just consumed at Wolf's Deli across the street, ritually washed down with a Dr. Brown's Cel-Ray. He was the kind of guy who talked in bellows and if you didn't seem to be paying attention to him, he'd hit you with the cane that kept his big body vertical. "Hey, kid! Howya doing?" he'd roar at me. Then he'd sit down at our phone and begin calling his gangster pals in Newark. Bob and I were sure that one day he'd get us arrested.

Although Teddy would hold court with his vivid tales of the stars he produced (which usually involved finding so-and-so nodding out in a bathroom stall, or falling asleep in the middle of a solo), he also had a weird sentimental side. One day, when I was running a customer-free store, Teddy—having no one to perform for—began telling me of his latest discovery, George Benson's pianist Jorge Dalto. "I want this album to be a hit," he told me gravely, "because I want to show my daughter that I'm not a bum." Sadly, the Dalto album tanked, as Dalto literally did a few years later, dying young of cancer. Teddy did live long enough to gain fame as Charlie Parker's producer.

Jazz, Etc. closed in '77. Bob had started to work for the newly revived Savoy label and decided to pack in the money-losing storefront. I was graduating from college and pondered momentarily the idea of taking it over, but never got past that first fleeting thought. Other things were percolating in my head: revolution, work, and getting out of my parents' basement. The possibility of becoming a Bernard Malamud-type shopkeeper didn't enter into the equation.

THE MAGNIFICENT THAD JONES /
BLUE NOTE 1546

"I'd rather hear Thad Jones miss one note
than hear Freddie Hubbard make ten!"
quipped Miles Davis, in a rare avuncular mood.

And here's Thad—alive once again—on Blue Note.
No predictable facts, no exclusions. Books me back
to William Paterson College's bare music room

and Thad's Friday lecture on "The Music." Young ears,
soft brain, naïve about the streets, sex and everything.

With Thad yelling
at the dreamers
next to the marimba:

"Does the name Tricky Sam Nanton
mean anything to you?"

THE WAY AHEAD

Listening to Archie Shepp's
Ben Websteresque mix
of yelps and dark acid
slaps me back to
the liner notes
anecdote of Shepp at
one of Albert Ayler's notorious
New Grass sessions
featuring Canned Heat's
Henry Vestine.

After the date, jazz's doyen
of Black Nationalism told
the hippie guitarist: "I would've
liked your playing a whole lot more
if I hadn't seen your face."

When I told this story
to Ted Berrigan over Budweisers
at the Grassroots Tavern, he wheezed
out some Chesterfield steam
& said: "If you think about
it, that's really a compliment,
though not a very friendly one."

DYSNOMIA

Waging war with myself
every weekday morning
but not out of anger
            it just gives me something to ruminate on
as I "make the coffee"
then strap on the daypack.

So Michael Ruby agrees with me:
"we" need to establish
a Trump-free zone in our brains
which X's out this piece.
No matter. Try again. Fart better.

I remember the knife inserted
into the soil
of a potted sansevieria
as my mother linked
with Ashkenazic folk ritual.

I prefer Eno's *Thursday Afternoon* among
his multiple stasis-inducers.

The global lifespan of the grimace

Confounded by the Chet Baker discography.
                                    —Oh just where does it begin
                                    & just how many
                                    "Last Concerts" did he give?
It gives me something
to think upon other

than the political
bad weather.
The Old Days of '77 back in Paterson
among the Chesterfield-smoking Maoists
the cable-spool table heavy with polemics & pamphlets
a simpler time on the Cold War barricades.

I put on an album of Gene Ammons' ballads for an answer get
none but that's all right
Gene had the human touch
in his tone and pace and
that's not as easy as you think
—try it in your daily life.

Someone else's favorite song is
just behind the door
I conduct a smile boycott at the workplace
but no one really notices.
Maybe it's not too late to
pick up smoking.

She told the table
that Jacques Derrida was a visitor to
her family's home in the 17th.

And he snuck cornichons off the children's plates and
asked her papa to play Don Byas LPs
insisting that the record's scratches, pops and skips were as
important as the music he was making.

"That's fucked up," said
the late Steve Dalachinsky to the above
on his way to a solo oboe recital.

I'm out the door, too, carrying a
container of chicken a la king
to no good purpose.

Comrades,
I am not doing my best.
György Lukács's home is now a
fixer-upper.
The pose of writing
sounds out in the chronic past
while a cop car's little blue lights skim off our
apartment's second floor windows.

Dysnomia is a learning disability that is categorized by a difficulty in remembering names or recalling words from memory needed for oral or written expressive language.

TO THE GREAT HARD-BOP PIANISTS

Club cloakroom as a soothing franchise, hats
for men lacking hats, and revise your face
as an authentic Mr. B collar ducks
beyond the reach of a dog-leg street.
I rap at the mystery door, nothing happens.
Phone ring: empty nest. I have all these friends
who keep accurate time.

The tone scientists have returned
from the lab. The reports came in from
the detective books. At home, Bobby Timmons' children
call him: "dear unpasteurized father of the depths."
At the Elysian Cafe's backroom, she told me
of Red Garland's last Dallas years
playing drunk boy requests.

Crushed Marlboros. Good tip in the ashtray. Old
sport jacket in an eye-blinking pattern.
Horace Silver runs from us in streams.
Wynton Kelly leaving a gig in a great dark jalopy.
The time machine's habit of summoning up Elmo Hope.
Everything can happen, even Ray Bryant.
Kenny Drew's nervous pulse across a cymbal's rim
—the light source for the hewed volumes of scrolls.

ALBERT AYLER AND BERNARD "PRETTY" PURDIE HAVE A LATE LUNCH, MANHATTAN, 9/5/68

Albert, he was all right!
—BERNARD PURDIE
(from an interview I conducted
for Mojo magazine)

There's no gain in being that *"Kid from yesterday,"* RIGHT?!?
It always begins with a mongrel piano . . .
& here I am broiling in azure leather pants
        and a vaselined face
that protects me from those Death Rays!
                                        and before Gort pays us a house call I'd
REALLY love to know the secret behind
your Purdie Shuffle . . . *pish-ship, pish-ship, pish-ship.*

You know, if I had Superman's power of flight, I wouldn't have to
take the bus any more. Hey, try some of my French Toast,
it's really great!

                                        especially with a big glass of ice-COLD buttermilk.

So, consider your capacity to fully surrender to
what I'm doing:
performing the music of abundance.
AND IT STEMS from a tradition that
demands respect.
Men like Junior "Shotgun" Walker demand respect. Men
like Rusty Bryant demand respect!

Cannonball Adderly utterly respected Rusty
and told me that he'd cut off his left nut just to
play half as good as Bryant
(or was that his RIGHT nut?)
I LOVE Rusty's LP *Friday Night Funk*
For Saturday Night Brothers
and when I place it on a turntable it
reminds me of moonrise
simmering over Cleveland.

Lame-ass sarcasm is the default mode of discourse in
this nada culture. *Do you know what I'm saying?* Thanks
for getting the check, I'll get it to you once Thiele comes
through with the royalties on *Love Cry.*

So you *still* want to know the mystery of my sound? Well
Bernard, I'm just trying to kill your god
and summon up the *spirit, the Neshama*
of Earl Bostic all at once, each
and every time I'm up on a bandstand biting
down on a #4 Fibercane reed.

"RED TOP"

"He collected unemployment,
ate potato knishes & played
at jam sessions"

Hubbub is the texture of stride.
Cigar smoking: a simple man's shtick.
Now a nod to Albert Ammons' troubled son
with the chatter from the bandstand
focused on a family whose forced smiles
match a piano lid's closing.

Soft press of Checkers
at the cabstand
in the November mizzle
as Gene "Jug" Ammons
fires his hapless drummer
beneath the atrium
of a green golf umbrella
adding some solid advice:

"It's delicate.
It's a cymbal, man.
It's not a jackhammer!"

THIRD VERSE

MY LIFE AS A JAZZ FAN
BOOK FOUR

After college, I made a stab at professionalizing myself by attending the New School's Urban Planning grad school. I had made friends at college with the social anarchist Murray Bookchin, whose little book on Urbanism, *Limits of the City,* had a big impact on me. I was going to be a humanist, Lewis Mumford-type Urban Planner who'd create the Livable City!—or something like that.

Unfortunately, a diagnosis of Type 2 diabetes derailed that particular train. Not that I was hospitalized or heavily medicated: I just sank into a realm between dysthymia and full-on depression. I withdrew from classes and hung around my parents' house listening to—what else—jazz LPs.

The one thing I managed to do was to start writing poetry far more seriously than I had in college. Back then, I had been all in for the Beats, especially Jack Kerouac, whose novel *On the Road* was for many the Gateway drug into jazz. Allen Ginsberg's poetry was laden with references to jazz and jazz musicians—his phrase "Bop Kabbalah" floated into the American language estuary. When *Howl* was published, Ginsberg trudged over to the Five Spot club to give Thelonius Monk a copy. The famed jazz pianist and "High Priest of Bop" was his idol. In a later encounter he asked Monk what he thought about the book. Monk's response: "Makes sense!"

My early attempts at poetry were more the product of killing time waiting for a bus—the damned fate of a commuting student without a car (perhaps an intimation of my calling, as the late William Matthews told me that the only adult males he knew without a driver's license were poets). The popular poetry models of the mid-'70s were Robert Lowell of the Boston Brahmin establishment Lowells, and Gary Snyder, a deep Zen poet with solid Beat connections and the caché of having been Jack Kerouac's inspiration for the character of Japhy Ryder in *Dharma Bums,* a popular book among campus literati. Snyder's Pulitzer Prize poetry collection *Turtle Island* was in high rotation, as was his prose book *Earth House-Hold.* However, what did I know of the atmosphere of Lowell's world of clubroom armchairs in Beacon Hill or Snyder's ecotopian vision, especially in a state where Superfund sites double as state parks? And did either of these poets ever write poems about going to the White Castle like I often did?

Maybe it's that depression is undervalued as an engine for creativity. All that rumination and self-involvement can lead to something. I found myself having writing sessions, not unlike what the jazz musicians call woodshedding, pounding away on my Precambrian-era Selectric typewriter, typing up drafts dutifully named Draft #1, Draft #2, and so forth. More importantly, I started seeking out other writers, hunting used book shops for poetry, and began organizing local readings, an activity where my training in left politics came in handy.

Listening to jazz, particularly jazz LPs, prepared me for my introduction to the arts. My copy of Ornette Coleman's landmark album *Free Jazz* featured a reproduction of Jackson Pollock's painting *White Heat* on the cover. I understood that Atlantic Records wanted to connect the audacity of this "action" painting with Coleman's radical challenge to chordal improvisation. Likewise, I received an introduction to art photography through the covers ot the Munich-based ECM Records. Owner/Producer Manfred Eicher featured some of Europe's best photographers, using images that hinted at what was awaiting the listeners. Rarely did the albums feature images of the musicians and they never used images of female models, a common art director's trope. I learned about modern graphic design through Reid Miles' Blue Note LP album covers, so iconic that they are often referenced or parodied by contemporary designers.

My initiation into the Sullen Art introduced me to the many contemporary poets who were also jazz fans. Like many devotees of that period, the first book about jazz that I read was Le Roi Jones' (Amiri Baraka's) *Blues People: Negro Music in White America,* one of the first books about jazz to be written by a black critic. *Blues People,* and the later sequel, *Black Music,* examined the social and cultural circumstances of jazz. They were also among the first books to look at the impact of John Coltrane and Ornette Coleman—other books that I read ended their studies with the hard bop that preceded them. When I later got to know Amiri, our discussions centered on jazz—not on the landmine territories of Maoism and Israel. I even interviewed him about John Coltrane for my low-rent mimeo magazine AHNOI!—wherein he noted that John Coltrane was a fan of *Blues People.* What I learned from Amiri's poetry was how he incorporated the rhythm and pulse of jazz into his sense of "the line"—that topic of endless conversation among contemporary poets.

Clark Coolidge, a prolific and highly original language-centered poet, not only was immersed in jazz but also was a jazz drummer who was active in his native Providence and kept playing drums throughout his life. We exchanged contact info after his reading at the Poetry Project and began a lively correspondence, mostly about jazz (Clark's side of the correspondence can be found in Yale's Beinecke Library). At some point, being young and without basic social coding, I invited myself to Clark's home up a mountain in the Berkshires. We stayed up late listening to Bud Powell albums. Clark's tastes in jazz were expansive, ranging from the early Dave Brubeck Quartets to Cecil Taylor. As my experience as a jazz listener was a solitary project—my friends either had little interest in the music that I loved or were just plain hostile—it was a pleasure to be able to talk both jazz and poetry.

601 LEXINGTON AVENUE

Warne Marsh Meets the Citicorp Tower & why not?
Found it at a Carteret collector's swap. B+ Condition,
the rare Japanese pressing
with alternate takes. With Marsh on tenor. Lou Levy on
piano, the great Peter Ind on bass,
Sandy "Teenbeat" Nelson on traps &
the white wedge tower
on baritone skyscraper. The album is filled with busy
rivulets of harmony and when the Citicorp Tower takes
the first solo on "You Stepped Out of a Dream" it has
the sheer sense of the release one gets
as the last seconds of a NPR pledge drive winds down.

But I really came on this soundstage
to tell the reader about power.
That I know nothing about it except
that I shouldn't
turn off the microwave
while the Keurig is brewing.

My slippered feet get
tripped by an extension cord
which makes me think again about
power in its most fundamental form:
keeping things on.

Meanwhile I putter between stabs at a poem
... not to mention Facebook posts that attempt to
pass myself off
as aimless, adroit & obstinate. This

is what I do too much.
Motivation: raise the incline already!
I'm judged adrift, transient, and no doubt
pointless in this jalopy sort of a world.

THE STAN GETZ QUARTET

1 "It Might as Well Be Spring"

The reporter
spoke to the homeless
Viet War Vet
in Lafayette Square about
living in the streets
of the capital.

"What gets me
through each day,"
he said, "are my cassettes
of Stan Getz. I *really* love
Stan Getz."

He then paused to
reconfigure
his response: "But, hey,
everybody loves
Stan Getz!"

2 "But Beautiful"

Stan Getz, at his best, seemed
to play his audience's dreams:
masculine lushness dappled with
Bay Rum cologne.

He also did interesting things,
like bringing the Bossa Nova
to pre-Beatles American ears,
canned sidemen who farted while
soloing and sticking up a Rexall's
with a water pistol.

The drug-addled Stan blew that heist as
the petite cashier ignored
the junk-jittery *goniff*
and waited on the wants
of an elderly Filipino gent.

But why worry that misdemeanor?
His "incredibly lovely sound" stays in the air of
this secessionist February morning.
It makes me think of Lucky Strikes,
the texture of gabardine
and cracked ice melting
in a finger-print marked snifter.

Asked by Edward R. Murrow
for the secret behind that "sound,"
Stan sighed as he replied:
"When I see things through my eyes,
I see things."

3 "I Let a Song Go Out of my Heart"

I knock at the mystery door and then it swings open:
Hey, it's Stan Getz in a lovely cantaloupe polo shirt
with the inevitable drink in hand, welcoming me in.

"You're Jewish right? I can tell. You've got that open smile."
Welcome to my *Mishpocheh,* Stan, with
Kenny Barron playing piano from the tape deck.

He shows me his latest album:
Stan Getz: The Business of Visitation
with Chet Baker on ham sandwich.
"It lies in so well with your interest in Gnosticism," I said.

The faint lettering of his air quotes seemed
like a geologic gesture: *"Beautiful things*
seem to come out of nowhere,
but they don't."

Stan Getz then doffs a smoking jacket
with a pineapple pattern
and while crushing out another Pall Mall,
he said in near murmur:

"Coltrane once said about me:
'Face it we'd all like to sound like that
if we could' but when I'm off I think
I don't want to be the Jewish Lester Young.'"

4 "Wrap Your Troubles in Dreams": Herb Alpert & Stan Getz go off to shul

It's 5749
According
to the kitschy Jewish
calendar Herb Alpert
nailed to a kitchen
wall, the sealed
& stamped letter
with his check
to the Chesed Food Bank
sitting on the marble counter.
"*I'm mailing it in for tzedakah,*" he tells his
wife, Lani Hall. "*Neil Sedaka
has money problems?*" she
responds, "*No, not Neil. It's
tzedakah, charity,
& I'm mailing it
on the way to Kol Nidre.*"

"*Hey! Can I get some more
matjes herring?*" That's Stan Getz,
plowing through the catered spread
from Nate and Al's. Getz's years of
living in Denmark with
a Swedish wife made him
something of a herring maven.
"*This is great, Herb!
It reminds me of Yom Tovs at Shelly Manne's
parents back in the '40s, except it's like
we are on a swanky movie set instead of
in a crummy Bronx apartment.*"

Alpert, a tailor's son
from LA's blue-collar Boyle Heights,
had become amazingly wealthy creating
pop music for '60s adults.
His band, The Tijuana Brass, was
like the Beatles for people
with mortgages & PTA Nights to attend. The Brass were
omnipresent: TV specials, commercials,
movie soundtracks, top ten hits, albums with racy photos.
"Now that's real music!" roared my Uncle Maish as
he put the needle down on
"Spanish Flea" for the 5th straight time during
a Sunday supper at their Ocean Parkway apartment.

Alpert and his partner Jerry Moss owned
A&M records, the largest independent record company
on the planet. Their label was immensely successful
recording a dizzying range of tastes—a stable of adult popsters
like the Carpenters, mega rockers The Police
& that dreamy Cat Stevens.

A&M's magic could put jazz on the pop charts! They took
Chuck Mangione, a hard bop trumpeter and rare
white face on a Jazz Messengers' bandstand and pulled
the #4 Billboard hit "Feel So Good" out of him. Alpert put
Gato Barbieri, a flame-throwing tenor saxist, atop
the Latino charts with the album *Caliente.*

Getz had signed with A&M after a decade of fine albums for
small labels that sold modestly. He and Alpert had just
finished recording *Apasionado*—a synth-laden return
to the Bossa Nova tunes that made Getz a pop star in
the pre-Beatle '60s.

Getz really needed the money.
He and his ex-wife had spent a decade
battling in divorce court.

He also had been given a terminal
diagnosis of liver cancer. He told drummer Mel Lewis:
"*I'm too evil to die*" and his powerful live performances led
some to believe that he'd sold his soul to the same *Gehenna*-
based agent that Robert Johnson used.

Alpert had his chauffeur drive him and Getz
to the magnificent Wiltshire Boulevard Temple, built
by the Hollywood moguls
of the '30s. The interiors were crafted by
movie set designers, so lavish
that it could be used as a soundstage
for a Technicolor biblical epic.

The pair arrived at shul a bit early, uncomfortable
in the grown-up bar mitzvah suits they were
wearing. Alpert was soon swarmed
by music industry types, a life hazard when one is worth a
billion dollars. A hipper segment of the congregation
plotzed seeing Getz near the pews instead of his usual
bandstand homeland. Few approached, given a history of
volatility. As friend Zoot Sims remarked, "Stan Getz?
A nice bunch of guys," and no one wanted to
ruin his *kavana* just before
the Gates of Repentance were flung open.

Now seated, fumbling
with his prayer books, just before
the Big Show got under way, Alpert adjusted his
brocaded yarmulke and asked the anxious Getz
about his trip to Israel a few years back
as a way of calming him down
before the long service. A light came on in
Getz's heavy lids as he told his pal: "*You*
know, Herb, when I'm playing,
I think of myself
in front of the Wailing Wall with

a saxophone in my hands, and
I'm davening, I'm really
telling it to the Wall!"

And as they rose together, along with
the rest of the congregation,
Getz whispered into his friend's right ear:
"I never played a note I didn't mean."

BUHAINA'S DELIGHT

I imagine the great
Art Blakey
in a too-tight suit
& thin mauve tie
straining inside
a stingy collar
mustering up
the thunder
in my Air Pods . . .

Bayonne Bridge
gorged in mist.
Wayne Shorter
playing the changes
put down by a foghorn,
while I sit like a *Golem*
trying to disinvest
from the whole habits
of a mind.

HOBOKEN HARD BOP ALERT

Can that be
the ghostly Red Garland
in the forward gloom?

Borsellino fedora lid at a bopper's angle.
The ancient micro-lapel sport jacket.
Tasseled oxblood loafers scraping an
approximate 4/4 rhythm
on the curbstone alley.

His flashlight: a lit DuMaurier that
illumines the pesky cylinder lock of
a Court Street front door.

CHARLIE HADEN REMEMBERS PAUL CHAMBERS

"I was watching Paul Chambers
to see if he had tears in his eyes.

It looked like he did.
He looked so great playing, man.

Then when the set was over,
he came right over to my table.

'Man, you are looking at me
the whole time!'

I told him my name,
and that I was a bass player

And that in every picture I'd
seen of him on stage

It looked like there were
tears in his eyes.

He looked at me for a moment, and
said, 'I do. I cry.'

I said,
'Man! That is so great!'

He asked to sit down
and we hung out for a minute.

Look at a picture of Paul Chambers.
Something about his features
is like somebody feeling
life very deeply.

Really Something."

SEIZE THE RAINBOW (IN MEMORIAM SONNY SHARROCK)

"You need your daily Coltrane"
—SONNY SHARROCK

"I consider myself a jazz saxophonist with a very
fucked-up horn. You know, the saxophone is such
a human instrument because you put your actual
breath into it & out it comes, the sound
comes out your insides, even if you are Anthony Braxton.

My mind is so full of what I'm hearing that I really don't
have the time or space to listen to anybody else, except
the Masters, who can always teach me.

. . . The brain is a very weird instrument.
So you should only listen to the shit
you like, because if you're listening
to a lot of bad shit
it'll come back on you
in the middle of the night
& you'll be helpless and powerless
to shut that shit off!!

You know, when I go out on stage,
my intention is to make
the first four rows
bleed from their ears."

THE PSYCHOGEOGRAPHY OF JOHN LEE HOOKER

"Yeah, Brady's was right off of
Gratiot Avenue.

Detroit was jumping then,
and Hastings Street
was the best street in town.

Everything you wanted was right there.

Everything you didn't want was right there, too!

It ain't no more now.
It's a highway now, called
Chrysler Freeway.

But that was a good street,
a street known all over the world."

JOHN LEE HOOKER & THE AMERICAN ECONOMY

"I did some as Johnny Williams.
I did some as Texas Slim.

Back in '49, I was hot as a firecracker!
        & they would give me **Big Money**
to do some material. So, I just used
my different names.

        I was *Texas Slim* for **King,**
John Lee Booker for **Chess**
        Johnny Williams for **Gotham**
The Boogie Man for **Acorn**
        Johnny Lee for **Deluxe**

& Birmingham Sam
        & His Magic Guitar
                for **Regent**

Money's pretty exciting y'know!"

SOURCE: Charlie Gillett: *Sound of the City.* New York: Pantheon, 1983 (Revised & Expanded Edition)

SOLOS

MY LIFE AS A JAZZ FAN
BOOK FIVE

Meanwhile, my knowledge of jazz made me employable in the era's "big box" record stores. Sam Goody's was a regional chain offering customers a deep selection of music, including a comprehensive jazz section. One day the redoubtable Teddy Reig wandered into the New Jersey branch store in Paramus where I was holding down a seasonal Christmas gig. When I told him that after Santa's imminent arrival I'd soon be hitting the streets, Teddy collared the store manager. He insisted that I be kept on. He bellowed, he banged his wooden cudgel, until the frightened manager agreed. It's good to have friends.

I was in charge of the jazz section. That included: gabbing with my fellow music-obsessed coworkers and handing out "courtesy" discount cards to attractive female customers (much in the manner of a fisherman putting a night crawler on his hook). But I also met singer Phoebe Snow and guitarist Al Di Meola, both of whom were searching for "what the kids are into." Local players would wander in and shoot the breeze and occasionally buy an album. I was a good up-seller of jazz—I was already familiar with a lot of the music in the sealed-up albums, and so sounded convincing about comparative quality.

At some point I noticed that many of the album jackets lacked information: it was the era of the gatefold, where the album opened like a wallet; inside would be two printed pages. These usually tightly printed pages gave you a lot of the stuff you really wanted to know—liner notes, personnel in the band, notes about the tunes, biographical information. So you had to buy the album and take off the cellophane to get at it.

Albums in the bins were put in plastic "inventory sleeves" with the album's name, the record label, and the catalog number. When you bought the album, the cashier took off the sleeve and put it in a box for the clerks who would then replenish the inventory.

In my role as jazz overseer, I took it upon myself—as a public service and for my own amusement—to write capsule descriptions of the albums, including a personnel listing, directly onto those sleeves. Sometimes, I had a little personal insider fun—on the cover photo for one of his albums, for example, the great sax man Sonny Rollins was sporting a full-on Mohawk. This was decades ahead of Punk fashion. Straight-faced, so to speak, I noted that the album contained a killer version of the swing-era warhorse "Cherokee." A couple of years later, after moving on, I returned to Goody's for a visit. These capsule notes had evidently proved popular with customers—I saw that my preview labels were still there, but written by someone else's hand. Evidently when the inventory sleeves wore out, someone recopied my little reviews, my first efforts at that game.

In my bachelor days I did go out to the Manhattan jazz clubs, but mostly by myself, given the deleterious effect such outings tended to have on my dating life. One cold night in February 1980, daring the fates, I took Doreen to see Cecil Taylor at the long-gone Fat Tuesday near Union Square. She was a really striking woman I knew from college. On the bandstand was a large ensemble (with two drummers). They played an intense set, one continuous performance later recorded and issued as "It Is in the Brewing, Luminous."

At the end, the whole audience, with one exception, exploded into applause and shouts. "That didn't sound much like Fleetwood Mac," Doreen mumbled, and that was the last time I saw her. No doubt she was at that point leery of any further adventures in the atonal wilderness. It reminded me of when I had taken my friend Ed, back in 1975, to see Anthony Braxton at the resurrected Five Spot. Ed and I had bonded around a mutual love of the Beats, but on this occasion he hated what he was hearing. What I think disturbed him more was that everyone else loved what they were hearing.

I loved going to the now long-vanished jazz clubs in the New Jersey suburbs. Near William Paterson there were two clubs within walking distance of each other on McBride Avenue, hard alongside the Passaic River. The Three Sisters featured members of the Thad Jones-Mel Lewis Orchestra, with Thad and Mel often playing in a quartet. Phil Woods and members of his working group also played there. The atmosphere was a bit clubby, and the groups up on stage seemed to be playing for their own amusement, rather than for the audience—something my rock-oriented friends picked up on when I cajoled them into joining me for a set. Did Mel Lewis really have to take a drum solo on a slow ballad?

Farther down the road was Amos Kaune's Gulliver's. Amos had run clubs in North Jersey for years. Gulliver's was hipper than the Sisters and brought in more contemporary players. I remember seeing tenor saxophonist Joe Farrell and trombonist Bill Watrous—hot players in the mid '70s. There was nothing fancy and the cover charge was 5 bucks plus a drink minimum. You could stay all night if you bought a drink for each set. The audience was a mix of older fans—the Paterson area was once a hot scene that produced singer Joe Mooney, guitarist Bucky Pizzarelli and pianist Al Haig—as well as young players who were studying with the many jazz musicians who lived in the area, along with the occasional civilian like me.

I continued along with my passion for the avant-garde fringe of the jazz scene, which went by many names: "Out Jazz," "Experimental Jazz," and "Free Jazz" were some of the terms that its devotees used. *"Turn that shit off!"* was the conceptual and critical term universally used by that music's detractors. None of the Midtown Manhattan clubs featured this music. The only advanced performer who regularly played clubs like the Village Vanguard was Cecil Taylor—his devoted following always assured a packed house.

A lot of the performances took place at galleries, art spaces or other one-shot venues. There was a great series at the Public Theater that featured many performers in tenor saxophonist David Murray's circle. It was easy to get to from the PATH train from Hoboken and, because it was held in a theater venue, I did not feel weird sitting there by myself.

One of my favorite spots was Verna Gillis's Soundscape, located in a loft on far West 52nd Street. I used to walk from the Port Authority for the 12 blocks along deserted 9th Avenue, prepared to get mugged before I got to hear some music. Once I arrived at 549 West 52nd, the Midnight Cowboy atmosphere shifted to one of music and art. The space was filled with the sculptures of Bradford Graves that doubled as musical instruments. The audience was convivial and the admission was well within my limited budget (and no drink minimums). It was even more intimate than the Jersey clubs; you sat on a folding chair and, if you desired, you could sit directly opposite the performers. Soundscape not only featured New York City-based players like guitarist Sonny Sharrock; Gillis brought in players from Europe, as well. It was thrilling to hear the expat soprano saxophonist Steve Lacy, whose LPs took up a serious chunk of my shelf space; however, I was bewildered that he had a pianist in his band and was playing more conventional material. I went up to him after a set (there was no dressing room for musicians to retreat to) and asked him about his shift in music. "Joel, I've played the music you've been hearing on my LPs for over twenty-five years. I thought it was about time to try something new." For an apprentice poet, it was a good lesson in active aesthetics.

AT J&R MUSIC WORLD
(SEPTEMBER 8TH, 2008)

I'm among the older men, so few
of us left now, shuffling among the bins
searching the innumerable extractions
of our musical time. The generic-to-my-ears hip hop
plays storewide; the record clerks are in ridiculous,
infantilizing smocks, stoically appearing hip.

Some guy enters J&R Music World,
asks the tough-looking female clerk leaning on the Beyoncé poster
"Do you have Country and Western cassettes?"
"No, we don't," she replies in a neutral tone.

"Where can I get Country and Western cassettes??",
"I don't know," the clerk says to the anxious guy,
"We haven't sold cassettes in years."
"Someone on the Brooklyn Bridge told me you sold them.
Why Was I Lied To?"

The clerk has run out of answers
"Sorry we couldn't help you, sir."

As he walks outside and onto Park Row he shouts,
"I Can't Afford A CD Player!"

From the back of the store—the Oldies Department—
someone yells out:
"Get With The Program!!"

aimed at us greybeards?
or at the departing guy
with a jones to hear
Little Jimmy Dickens
spooling about on mylar?

All I know is this—
in this land of nonstop playthings
they're changing the numbers on me.

WE TRAVEL THE SPACEWAYS

ON THE BANDSTAND WITH SUN RA

Trombonist Julian Priester nabs
a tiny dumpling of air
sending it back minus wet lungs
to the interior hunger of a people
scribing their history through sound's destiny.

John Gilmore shapes his tenor solo like harm unlikely
to escape from the American house of folly.
It's really just a shrug against a culture
of neatly stacked dollars. *"I do not waver,*
I am one voice," he whispers
to altoist Danny Davis.

"Why of course it made sense," Davis recalled,
"I mean, *I'm* a tone scientist, too!"
Then—February 12, 1981—he swore me to silence,
by the cutout bins of J&R Music World,
across from the mumblers inside City Hall Park.

"GLORIA'S STEP"

Someone at the Vanguard's back tables
is muttering about Jack Paar
and that *"The colored bartender is watering
down the drinks"*

and even through Air Pods
you can hear the drink-ice crack to maps
between the notes in Bill Evans' solo.

"That's where I'm going—there's plenty of THAT*"*
says a husky female voice riding over the splay
of Paul Motian's Zildjians. Preservation act

from an age of pillbox hats direct to today's Manhattan,
where manatees now swim up the Hudson.

And only the savagely sweet faces of privileged daughters
remain to hold back the advancing continent.

ALGIERS, LOUISIANA

It seems perfect, muted
as a prayer gorgon,
and the rim of the city across the river
was a crescent of RC Colas
and melting Moon Pies.
Faulty CD player turns the Meters into John Cage.
Day-Glo bird roosts near the Necco-colored tanks.
This is where I invest the habits of my wrist
and, on this swath of levee, krewe floats
became tips of joy for schoolkids on holiday.

It wasn't in my cards, though, palming
hot sauce in lieu of talisman.
My planet is a crib whose orange juice is gaunt.
I break bread with a goat who knew Monk.
I don't know anything but the sources.
I check my watch to see when the doodads hatch.
I have all these rivers running through my shirt.

BIRTH OF THE COOL

We enter a magic magazine to see
Miles Davis' Nonette at the Royal Roost
playing Johnny Carisi's "Israel" on lit cigarettes.

Rain across Duffy Square, no moon nightlight
& the papaya vendors' luau hats have become
soaked clumps of hemp. Now reckless
in the dim room; not a subscriber to nostalgia,
but trust in a renewal of things.

And after the gig: the broken white lines jump
in front of Lee Konitz as he drives
home in a red jalopy on the road past
the Tootsie Roll factory.

SESSIONOGRAPHY

Tonight I cannot sing, but fear to weep
so I doff a Mister B collared shirt
to balm my nerves & nerves they are & they've
been that way, generations even, back to
my *Galitzianer* forerunners
sullenly tending to a sorrel patch.

& what do I really know from Ben Webster
except that he enjoyed beating people up
which gained him the nickname "Brute,"
though by his *schnapps*-heavy Copenhagen dotage
he wept lakes just thinking about
"Mother," earning him a tag
that was Danish slang for "big old crybaby."

Ben Webster & I share the same yearning
for uncluttered melodic improvisation
except that my axe is a fountain pen
filled with peacock-blue ink.

Jersey-bound, I rise up from a subway *Gehenna*
& spy a Reality Star tearing up
in a Chambers Street Dollar Store. And it makes me think
back to that Scandinavian night when "the Brute"
handed a kid Archie Shepp a box of Rico Royal Reeds
complete with the stern admonition:
"*Kid, get some more vibrato!*"

A CONDUCTOR OF ENERGIES

"I was a pretty good bebop drummer
then Cecil Taylor came along
and ruined me."

In the sunset of ofay paralysis
you hear Sunny Murray's
barrier-free drumming
and think to yourself:
"*time to take up something practical*"
then one's emptied head
runs out into rush hour traffic
like a Tex Avery character.

Murray is nonplussed
and must own a particular pain
behind those round lens shades.
The legend was that he packed heat
to insure payment at a gig's end.

Reverie has a class bias. Then
add to that the glaze of omission
and treated as less
than foot traffic.

Smoking between sets,
counting the small house
with a car alarm outside
insisting. Sunny and his band
ready for the last number.
Late night's involuntary
incognito brotherhood.

AFTER HEARING THE LEE KONITZ TRIO

Shutter phase of Manhattan's nightwork
& the Church Street post office is cluttered with night mailers.
Shade of terrific things shadowed
by the pulseless surge of memory.
Eighteen years ago, Paterson,
in the loft above an IGA market.
"Silk City" ran on minimal efficiency.
And we allowed ourselves nothing of the future.
The music came from somewhere there
and sounded like the back-up band for the Drifters. Nothing
was determined, you were about to go out
and among your heads, your prodromal weather let me read
"vivacious" instead of madness.
Night throb Passaic go-go bar thunk
squanders the recall of "then" the drift
of a "where are they all now."
I last heard from you in a not-needed call
ten years back as the Weehawken air pebbled
with drifting saucer magnolia petals. Not enough
patience with myself, no emotional capital to spare
for the ever-changing economy of insanity.

CHATTING WITH ZAVATSKY

"*Paul Bley???* Man—
I hate him! He does
NOTHING for me.
I saw him play
with Lee Konitz
at the Jazz Standard

& he was in his
own world. A bad
evening.

              . . . but guess who
I've been listening to lately?

 . . . *Richard Twardzik*!

                        —do you know him?"

BACK TO THE HEAD

MY LIFE AS A JAZZ FAN
BOOK SIX

Well, what does one do with a brainpan overflowing with the effluvia of years of reading liner notes, jazz histories, *downbeat* and *Rolling Stone* magazines, participating in record store aisle bull sessions and in-between-set conversations with the makers of the music? I began writing about it.

I must admit to having a timeshare in the Impostor Syndrome co-op. I can't play an instrument, never took a lesson, and have only a faint knowledge about the chassis that runs the music machine. Realizing this gap in my cultural kitbag, I had taken a Music Appreciation class while at William Paterson. The teacher was a nice guy; he bragged that he went to DePaul University with the band Chicago's horn section, and would play (for the dreamers in the back rows) sections of the soundtracks for the porn films he scored in order to supplement his adjunct's salary—and maybe it ties in with my Battle Royal with mathematics, but the basics of music were a torture rack. The teacher took *rachmones* (compassion) on me and gave me a mercy "C" in exchange for a Singers Unlimited LP that I special-ordered from Jazz, Etc.

Focusing on the placement of music in its cultural, social, and historical setting was my go-around. I began my music journalism in college by interviewing Bucky Pizzarelli, who taught at WPC, and using my connections with Bob Porter to interview guitarist Pat Martino, a hero of mine. I sat through hours of a rehearsal for an important gig that was not going well. It was a lesson for me in how music gets put together. Afterwards, Martino sat down with a twenty-year-old college journalist and was patient and open. I suppose he was also surprised that I was conversant with his entire musical career.

After college, I wrote a lot for the Jewish presses, especially the newly-launched English language version of the venerable Yiddish paper, the *Forward*. As long as there was a Jewish angle, I could pitch a story. I interviewed rock music's Zelig, Al Kooper. Kooper's career ranged from playing organ on Dylan's "Like a Rolling Stone" to discovering, then producing, the southern rock band Lynyrd Skynyrd—not to mention founding (and then quitting) the horn-based Blood, Sweat and Tears—and of course forming the Blues Project. When I interviewed him in 1994, Kooper had just released *Rekooperation,* his first album in years, having been for a while semi-retired, thanks to songwriting credits that included "This Diamond Ring," made famous by Gary Lewis and the Playboys in 1965. When Kooper signed his first publishing deal, the company owner told him, "Your songs are like your children; they'll come back and take care of you when you're older."

Kooper's cranky persona reminded me of some of my uncles, except that he started the Blues Project instead of an accounting firm. He also gave me a Jewish "sweet spot" that sold the story to my editor at the *Forward:* I told him that Kooper had said to me, "Mike Bloomfield told me, that 'the reason Jews are attracted to the Blues is that Jews suffer internally, and Blues is all about external suffering.'"

Before we concluded the interview, I revealed to Kooper that when I'd attended Yeshiva, we sang the daily prayer *"Yigdal,"* to the melody of "This Diamond Ring." Our deeply Orthodox teachers were befuddled, but found my friend Moishe's explanation reasonable: "It's a Sephardic melody I learned when I was in Israel." They were also, no doubt, impressed by the energy we put into that old Hebraic warhorse.

"Hey, man, sing it for me!" Kooper exclaimed. And, on command, I did. "Hey, man," he responded, "that sounds cool. I shoulda paid more attention to my rebbes!"

I do take some credit for helping to promote the new wave of Klezmer music that was brewing in the cities of the Northeast. My editor at the *Forward,* Jonathan Rosen, gave me the stink-eye at my initial pitch, but the newly emergent scene was hard to ignore within the Jewish cultural community. In particular, I wrote a number of pieces about the Klezmatics, who brought a "downtown" aesthetic to the music, which included being queer-friendly and with cheeky album titles like "Jews with Horns" and "Rhythm and Jews." I was in attendance at Radio City Music Hall for a sold-out concert featuring Itzhak Perlman and the *crème de la schav* of the Klezmer scene.

I even brought my parents along to the event. At the reception afterwards, I introduced my folks to the musicians. My Auschwitz survivor father, unenthused by this music of the *shtetl* culture he'd grown up in, got impatient and exclaimed, "Nu, when is Perlman coming out?" I had to explain that a post-concert repast for the great violinist would probably not include cheese cubes and vegetable sticks.

I wrote for other publications as well. In the days before Internet culture, you could phone up an editor and pitch a story. Which was what I did for the very short-lived *Seven Days* magazine, when I heard that Moondog, the blind street musician dressed in robes and topped with a Viking helmet, was coming to play a concert at the Brooklyn Academy of Music. Moondog had been a New York City personality in the '50s and '60s, reciting his poetry and playing his self-invented percussion instruments. In 1974, he disappeared off his accustomed location at the east side of 6th Avenue between 53rd and 54th Streets, where he'd once chatted with Charlie Parker and the other musicians who played in the clubs of 52nd Street. Bob Porter assured me that Moondog was dead, and that I was going to meet "some fake Moondog." But when I got to the hotel on lower Lexington Avenue, I was confronted with the genuine article, sans robes and helmet. He told me that he'd gone to Europe to perform some concerts and stayed on. It was his manager who convinced him to update his wardrobe, so as to be taken more seriously as a composer. Which the European audiences did, and the last decades of his life were filled with performances and recordings.

Years later, I gave a reading of my Moondog profile in a Reykjavik record store called 12 Tonar. Icelanders, many of whom are descendants of the individuals named in the Norse sagas, *love* Moondog, no doubt because of the composer's devotion to the Old Norse religion and gods like Odin. Apparently, chess players do also—as I was leaving, Johannes, the shop's owner, said, "Do you know who was watching you read? Bobby Fisher!" The chess genius had found refuge in Iceland when no other country would take him in because of the radio broadcasts he had made praising the 9/11 attacks; the proviso was that he would refrain from his crazy, Anti-Semitic and just plain Anti-Whaddaya-Got rantings. Johannes added that he often saw Fisher wandering the streets of the city and, no, he didn't think Fisher was a Moondog fan.

My longest sustained period writing about music began in 2002 when one of my wife's old students joined the publicity department of the New Jersey Performing Arts Center (NJPAC) in Newark. NJPAC was part of an ambitious project that brought a minor league baseball stadium, luxury housing, a light rail extension, and a performing arts center to downtown

Newark. After a bad experience hosting a hip-hop concert in the inaugural season, the NJPAC management began focusing on musical forms whose fans would treat the facility more gently—which brought a stream of jazz performers to the main stage.

Most of my interviews for NJPAC were "phoners." I would talk to a publicist, who would give me the performer's phone number and a time to call. I would do an interview with eyes on "pull quotes" as part of the profile that would be included in the program handed out to concert goers. The musicians I was talking to had moved up from club work to the concert hall and were familiar with this part of the publicity process. Most were surprised to be interviewed by a real live jazz nut, rather than someone who had gleaned his/her info from a Wikipedia entry.

These interviews also opened my jazz world view, which at that time still favored the extreme edges. Some of my early jazz mentors represented what might be called a bizarre perversion of Black Nationalism—white fans who viewed with deep suspicion anything possessing the soupçon of a melody and/or a chord progression. So, there I was, interviewing Dave Brubeck, a particular object of scorn for my sunglasses-at-night mentors. But Brubeck was great to talk to and was even aware of *In His Own Sweet Way: Tribute to Dave Brubeck,* which John Zorn had produced for a Japanese label and which featured a group of all-stars from the Downtown music scene. "Man, they were really far-out versions of my tunes," he said with a laugh. Apparently, Dave dug our interview, because he had Columbia hire me to do the liner notes for the *Essential Dave Brubeck* compilation. It was the most money I ever got for writing about music.

And I interviewed pianist Ramsey Lewis, who'd had a string of top ten pop hits in the early '60s, and who remained a popular concert attraction. I asked whether he ever got tired of playing his very popular version of Dobie Gray's "The In Crowd." His reply was brusque: "There might be someone coming to one of my concerts for the first time after listening to my music since he's been a youngster. How could I *not* play 'The In Crowd' for him?"

One day, while I was doing all these phoners, the call came to interview Ornette Coleman. This was different—I decided that I had to meet him in person. My editor wangled a phone number from someone for James Jordan, Ornette's cousin and manager. When I called him, he was hesitant about an in-person interview. I unloaded a cartload of reasons—made up as I went along—which persuaded him to take one more step. He passed my request on to Ornette's son Denardo, who had worked closely with his dad since he was a pre-teen, and was now Ornette's drummer and producer.

At the time I was a social worker (my day job) at a truancy reduction center. The cops would pick up the young loiterers and put them in our center, until their usually furious parents came to redeem them and return them to school. My day was over, and I was waiting for a bus when Denardo called. I told him I knew his mother, Jayne Cortez, as we were both published by *Hanging Loose Press.* I then mentioned (as part of my logistics planning) that the interview needed to be done in the late afternoon because of my social work gig. "My wife," said Denardo, "is a social worker, too!" Touchdown! We promptly set up a time for me to meet his father.

Ornette's loft was in the Garment District, a short walk from the Port Authority bus terminal. James Jordan greeted me at the elevator door. The space was airy and well-lit and filled with art. When Ornette came in and introduced himself, I had to push teenage Joel back down inside and perform as adult Joel. Ornette was dressed in an amazing multi-colored silk outfit, more appropriate for the royal court of Sun Ra's home planet Saturn than for the urban charivari of West 40th Street. I later read that all of Ornette's clothes were bespoke and that he wore a new outfit every day.

Interviewing him was a tougher task than I had imagined. He talked obliquely; it was hard to get straight answers to softball questions. As for his near-decade absence from performing and recording, he revealed no more than that he was traveling and "listening to new things." However, when I asked him what album listeners unacquainted with his music should listen to as an introduction to it, his answer was quick: *Skies of America,* the 1972 album where Ornette improvises over a notated score performed by the London Symphony Orchestra. This album divided his fanbase, as it stood in stark contrast to his previous more open style. Its high production costs were probably the reason that Columbia Records dropped him not long after the record's release. In my home alcove workspace, next to my photos of Ted Berrigan and Charles Olson, is the one my wife took of me and of Ornette backstage at NJPAC. What would teenage Joel make of that?

I'm not going to say that jazz is my religion, as Ted Joans did—I think too much of it to surround it with a church (or *shul*). I wish I had learned an instrument, even a melodica, but my formal laziness scared me away from the scales and practice that go with it.

I don't hear "Is jazz dead?" as much as I used to. It has a presence in the culture that it didn't have when I was a kid. More sophisticated pop-music fans know who Miles Davis, John Coltrane, Thelonius Monk, and Bill Evans are. There is a sizeable number of crossover jazz acts—like Diana Krall, Esperanza Spalding, and Chris Botti—who appear at PACs and the many regional jazz festivals that have emerged in recent years. The expansion of jazz programs around the country guarantees not only a flow of well-educated jazz musicians, but also jobs for the older mentors who teach them. It's an international music now, with many countries producing talented performers who often train at U.S. schools or at the many jazz programs that exist around the world. When I attended the Copenhagen Jazz Festival a few years back, I was struck that not only were there no American performers, but also, most of the acts came from northern Europe. I finally understood Phil Woods' complaint when I had interviewed him for an NJPAC profile that "Work is drying up for me in Europe!"

"STEP LIGHTLY"

Debark off the Paterson-bound train to
see Williams's Garrett Mountain
looming huge as an umber Mallomar
with those WPA stairs plunging into a city where
people have given up on space
to put their money on living through time.

A panhandler tries out a fresh take
on this new *arrivant:* "Can you help me out?
I need 63 cents to get to the Garden State Plaza
and nobody here speaks English!"
A beggar in a strange land gets himself a frog skin.

The man in Paterson who can buy his children
Happy Meals & still has change in his pocket is a
little aristocrat & with that insight filed away I
charge up on Cianci Street cappuccino,
tip my derby to the Lou Costello statue
then stride uphill towards the Great Falls.

No little lyric miracles today.
Boxing Day celebrated someplace else in the world
and could that be Clifford Brown's "Sandu" blaring
from the speakers of a brown Oldsmobile idling by
the entrance to Libby's Lunch?

WOULDN'T YOU AGREE?

This Journal Square of
non-working
ornamental fountains,
fenced-in parks,
dull office buildings.
"Kennedy Fried Chicken" joints
now seems populated
with trial members
of some sketchy dating services
stalking potential
meet-up sites.

An imposing woman
in Robert Crumb pumps strides
past me along
Sip Avenue's slate sidewalk clutching
a pocketbook made of cork.
I think: *"What happens when it rains?"*
recalling Portugal's *cartiça amedia.*

I then think I ask myself too many
Walking Encyclopedia-type questions
all the time, wherever I am
and to no one's amusement.
That stern poet Armand Schwerner
        once admonished me:
"Life is not a punchline"
while he shoved back
a sheaf of my poems as if it was dosed
in cooties.

Every place I've been
wherever I've had "neighbors"
or "co-workers," I'm considered
an intruder, a stranger, "a Jew."
I'm always eating lunch by myself on a bench.
I'm always "presenting my papers."

And there's no "vocal fry" no "uptalk" to
enliven my ears as I trek among
the luckless pedestrians
joining me in the silent
urban cakewalk
to government offices & medical clinics
—my own hajj is to the NJ DMV
to replace a state ID
lifted in Pessoa's Lisbon.

I try to retain my predilection for mutiny.
Convince myself that I want to try skydiving,
spelunking, rock climbing, sailplaning, getting
blasted out of a cannon
or voting Republican.

But the light changes and here I go
crossing Summit Avenue into
the standard dreary "Motor Vehicles"
of many forms and snaking lines.
Oh for theatrical atmospheric magic! None here,
the in-house ozone heavy with unhappiness.

The waiting room bleeds from "Oldies":
Toto, Bachman-Turner Overdrive,
"Colour My World." The Captain
AND Tennille. Gene Pitney.
The increments of human life
measure in horsefly crap
. . . it's gotten to that.

And then out of the surrounding
pond of faces someone is calling me
—"Joel! JOEL!!"
not the usual "Joe!"
or that sardonic
Garden State salute
"HEY! YOU! ASSFACE!"

The Village Caller in question?
—Jacob Burckhardt, not that
real-dead historian
but a son of Rudy B.
& friend to many
of my "downtown" friends,
but now a *landsman*
In this land of stink bombs
and vacant bodegas.

He: "After 12 years here,
I thought it was time to get a Jersey license."
Me: "I got pickpocketed in Lisbon."

Our mutual presence celebrates the
monotony of this place—
has anyone ever written a poem, haiku, or
limerick about a DMV office
until this inky Mutoscope?

Finally, the cinema of inertia concludes
& I wallet the proof text of who-I-am to-"them."
But the emigrant, Jewey feel lingers.
while the convulsive network spindles on
with the Boxtop's "The Letter" serving
as a pencil point of sound.

To Whom It May Concern:
Lock the lock when leaving.

But first: adieu & a question to my still
entrapped-on-line brother culture worker:
"Jacob, who do you most admire,
dead or alive, rumor or myth?"

He replied, while looking past me, & toward the
breaking sunlight outside:

"Pigeons.
—Because *nothing*
fazes them."

THE ORIGINS OF MY SOCIAL MARGINALIZATION

12 minutes countdown
    to the 8:15 St. George boat
so walk over to
    that enormous Starbucks
at Pearl & State.
    Inside, I hear that sinuous flute break
from "California Dreaming"
    dripping from the sound system
then think *"that's Bud Shank."*
    —he a magus of West Coast jazz,
later a first call studio stalwart
    who could read
"fly shit on staff paper."
    The ultimate kudo among his peers.
I then realize
    how cursed I am with a particular
knowledge which sets me
    apart from co-workers, neighbors
& August's luckless latte sippers
    who listen to the same canned goods
thinking: "that's The Mamas & The Papas"
    & see a brain kinescope
of Michelle Philips in a miniskirt.
    I then realize myself
doubly cursed and estranged
    aware that the present
row of State Street's
    post-modern towers
were once rooming houses
    for my *landsmen*

cleared for entry
                    & hot off the Ellis Island ferry
spending their first night
                    alone in this drab New World.

"I DIDN'T KNOW WHAT TIME IT WAS"

Tabloid grey December aboard
The Governor Lehman and after 25 minutes
of dodging tugs & tankers across
Upper New York Bay, the ferry wins its
battle with the current,
docking into St. George Slip #2.

Pudding-head me spent the trip napping
to Dave Brubeck—he's squarer than Ajax
but, at 82, still on the hustings of jazz.
Once a collegiate ideal & an unsung daddy
to prog-rock, he supplied the cracked chord
strata for the still missed Paul Desmond.

Headphones on: I greet
poet-stowaway Lee Ann Brown,
off to proctor an exam up
on Grymes Hill. Reaching into
an indigo duck bag,
she offers up a tangerine
—the last song I played
by Brubeck has now
actualized. I accept the gift, then
rush to the 44 Yukon Avenue bus,
Platform "D."

"I REMEMBER CLIFFORD"

As I order my overpriced small coffee
at Whitehall Terminal's Central Market
I look up at the encyclopedic menu board
noticing that this humble commuter's spot
offers truffle oil fries to its undemanding clientele.

With those delicate spuds nesting in an off-white bag
I walk off of Manhattan, that island of total theft,
where everything you see is stolen
or just seized because it can be.

My head is on wrong again, so counterbalance
with headphones privatizing the genius
of the Clifford Brown and Max Roach Quinter.

Starting to doze as the ferry passes Governors Island,
I dream up a shout-out: *"Brownie, don't get
into that car!"* for about the 89th time
since 1973 with that hurt wish
once again balmed by sentiment.

THE RUMPROLLER

Let the Zoomers drool while
the Ferryboat Marchi passes
the last risible chunk of
Governor's Island, then
straight into the pea-soup brume.
The passengers on the hurricane deck
shouting into smart phones
"WE'RE BREAKING UP!!"
with the focus
on reception
not relationships.

We've just left
the reach of scar city,
that never healed city, city
of too many high-end donut quays, unhappy
waitresses and sulking doormen who imagine
their better lives
removing water from the floor
of the Indian Ocean.

And if you're asking,
I'd rather be where the doodads hatch
instead of this failed venture in stylizing
my Kairite-lite life. I just
want to talk about everything
that has happened to me
so far, but there's too much of that going
around already. The referee calls a
time-out and Spotify gives me trumpeter

Lee Morgan to work with, neatly
packaged inside
the light constancy of things.

"THE THEME"

(Semi-Buddhist)

I imagine Art Blakey
in a too-tight dark suit
and stingy collar
mustering up
the thunder
in my headphones.
Ammann's Bayonne Bridge cloaked.
in pea-soup mist as Hank Mobley
plays the changes off
the ferry house foghorn
while I try to disinvest
from the whole habits of my mind.

FINAL BAR

One aspect of my jazz history closed when Bob Porter died on April 10th, 2021. I was pleased by the extensive obit in *The New York Times* and that he had become such a well-known figure in the musical world. His passing was covered on many media platforms, all noting his two Grammys and five Grammy nominations. I had kept in touch to the extent that I'd frequently call Bob when I needed a quote for an article or some information to track down a source. And once, on a plane to New Orleans with my wife to attend one of her film conferences, I looked across the aisle and there was Bob! Aloof as always, he said, "Hi!" as if it had been a week, not 15 years, since we'd seen each other. After a few minutes of pleasantries, he looked at me and said grimly, "Hey, Joel, are you still listening to that goddamned avant-garde shit?"

SAFETY
ZONE
NO PARKING
HOTEL
SAFETY
ZONE

PHIL WOODS

"DRIFTING ON A REED"

"After my friend Hal Serra and I took our lessons from Lennie Tristano in Queens,
    we'd routinely take the subway into Manhattan
        to get a pizza
            or a nice bowl of spaghetti
                & a Coca-Cola   for 25 cents
                    at Romeo's, on Times Square.

Romeo's was a dying chain
but you knew the pasta was good
because there was a big vat of it
sitting in the window all day,
. . . al dente was *not* in our vocabulary then.

One time after a lesson Lennie said,
'Are you guys going down to 52nd Street?'
We said: 'Yeah, why do you ask?'
Lennie said: 'I'm opening for Charlie Parker.
I thought you might like to meet him.'
I said to myself, 'Yeah, I've always wanted to meet God.'

The Lennie Tristano Trio opened,
& when they were through,
the bassist, Arnold Fishkin, came to get us.

So Arnold and Lennie took us behind the curtain
and there, sitting on the floor,
was the great Charlie Parker
eating a cherry pie.

He said, 'Hey kids, you want a piece of cherry pie?'
I said, 'Oh Mr. Parker, cherry is my favorite flavor!'

I've always loved cherry pie.

So he cut me a big slab,
and we talked music.

We were there for 5 or 10 minutes.
Then he had to go to work.

He had his pie,
then the lesson started.

We went back outside
and listened to an hour
of the genius of the alto saxophone."

2.

"I had just graduated
from Juilliard in 1952

and found myself playing
at the Nut Club on Sheridan Square.

After that great education
here I was playing "Harlem Nocturne"
ten times a night.

I wasn't happy with myself. I
didn't like my mouthpiece. I
didn't like my reed.
I didn't like my horn.
I didn't even like my strap!

One night,
somebody came into the club and said:
'Charlie Parker's playing across the street at
Arthur's Tavern. He's jamming!'

I was going on my break, so I rushed over.
When I walked in, there was
this 90-year-old guy playing a piano
that was only three octaves long!

And there was an even older geezer on drums
playing a tiny snare
and using tin pie plates for cymbals!

And there was the great Charlie Parker
—playing a baritone sax!
(It belonged to Larry Rivers, the painter)
Parker knew me. He knew all the kids coming up
so I said, 'Mr. Parker, perhaps you'd like to play my alto?'

He said,
'Phil, that would be great.
This baritone's kicking my butt!'

So, I ran across the street to the Nut Club
and grabbed the alto saxophone that I hated.

I came back and got on the bandstand,
which was as big as a coffee table.

I handed my horn to Bird
and he played "Long Ago and Far Away."

As I'm listening to him playing *my* horn,
I'm realizing there's nothing wrong with it.

Nothing was wrong with the reed.
Nothing was wrong with the mouthpiece.
Even the strap sounded good!

Then Parker says to me, 'Now you play . . .'

I said to myself, 'My God.'
So I did.
I played a chorus for him.

When I was done,
Bird leaned over and said,
'Sounded real good, Phil.'

This time
I levitated over Seventh Avenue
back to the Nut Club.

And when I got back on the bandstand,
I played the SHIT out of "Harlem Nocturne."

That's when I stopped complaining
and started practicing.

That was quite a lesson."

3.

"One late afternoon I was in Charlie's Tavern, a big
musician's hangout on 51st Street off Seventh Avenue.

Someone comes into the bar and says:
'Bird is riding down Seventh on a horse!'

We all go outside and there is Bird
on a white Palomino horse
wearing his straight fedora
and a pinstripe suit.

I yelled out, 'Hey Charlie, how you doing?'
He said,
'I'm going to break my ride
and get a meatloaf sandwich.'

(That's what you ate at Charlie's Tavern.
You had a meatloaf sandwich and a beer.)

After he finished eating, all of us kids
followed him back out to the street to his horse.

We said 'Bye-bye Charlie' as
he rode off into the sunset.

Who *was* that masked alto saxophone player?"

Acknowledgments

Some of these poems first appeared in: *Big Hammer, Connections New York City Bridges in Prose and Poetry (*eds. Peggy Garrison and David Quintvalle, P&Q Press), *Moment's Notice: Jazz in Poetry and Prose* (eds. Art Lange and Nathaniel Mackey, Coffeehouse Press), *No Placebos, Ribot, Surrender When Leaving Coach (*Hanging Loose*), Shuffle Boil, Veritas* and *Vertical's Currency: New and Selected Poems* (Talisman).

An earlier version of the memoir section "My Life as A Jazz Fan I" appeared in *Jerry Jazz Musician* (www.jerryjazzmusician.com).

A tip of my somewhat battered porkpie hat to the crew at Hanging Loose Press, especially my erstwhile editor and fellow digger Dick Lourie for his guidance in shaping this book, as well as Art Editor Elizabeth Hershon for helping obtain permission for the use of the cover art and the photograph used within the volume.

Much thanks for Pat Ethridge for typing the manuscript and adding needed changes and deletions over the months . She can now recite whole sections of *Well You Needn't* from memory.

And, of course, once again much thanks and love to my wife Sandy Flitterman-Lewis for her close reading of my work, setting me straight on the basics of grammar (the bonus for marrying an English professor), tolerating my minority taste in music and being my partner in life here on the west bank of the Hudson.

Liner Notes

ALBERT AYLER (1936–1970) A tenor saxophonist from Cleveland, with roots in Rhythm and Blues, gospel saxophone and military band music, Ayler developed an approach to jazz that blasted through the door opened up by Cecil Taylor (whom he played with), Ornette Coleman and John Coltrane (who encouraged Impulse records to sign him to the label and who requested on his death bed that he play at his funeral). Coltrane's late ecstatic style was directly influenced by his younger protégé. The poem "Albert Ayler and Bernard 'Pretty' Purdie Have a Late Lunch . . . " plays off "To Mr. Jones—I Had a Vision," a visionary testament written by Ayler and published in 1969 in *The Cricket: Black Music in Evolution*, edited by Amiri Baraka, Larry Neal and A.B. Spellman.

Spiritual Unity (ESP-Disk)
Witches and Devils (Freedom)

BIX BEIDERBECKE (1903–1931) The patron saint of hard-core classic jazz fans, cornetist Beiderbecke, self-taught and unable to read music, played with a laconic precision and harmonic sophistication that anticipates Miles Davis; he performed across a range of regional bands before landing a spot with the very popular Paul Whiteman Orchestra. His brief, tragic life has been the subject of much musicological and biographical research; the book, and subsequent movie, *Young Man With A Horn*, is partially based on his life.

Bix Beiderbecke and The Chicago Cornets (Milestone)
At the Jazz Band Ball (Columbia)

ART BLAKEY (1919-1990) A drummer of enormous power and great subtlety, Blakey was one of the developers of the "hard bop" idiom, which drew inspiration from both gospel and rhythm and blues and sought to broaden bop's coterie audience. His group, the Jazz Messengers, was an international attraction and a training ground for players ranging from Lee Morgan to Wayne Shorter to Wynton Marsalis. The poem "Buhaina's Delight" is taken from an LP title which itself references the name Blakey took when he converted to Islam.

Moanin' (Blue Note)
A Night In Tunisia (Blue Note)

THE BRILL BUILDING SOUND: The poem "Wasn't Born To Follow" is a nightmare romp inspired by reading the liner notes of a boxed CD collection called The Brill Building Sound. This building, located 1619 Broadway, was the epicenter of American pop music from the late '50s to the mid–'60s; that is, the interregnum between the plane crash that killed Buddy Holly ("The Day the Music Died") and the arrival of the Beatles. By 1962, there were 162 music related businesses in the building—one could write a song, pay for arrangements, record a demo with the many musicians who could be found in the halls and then pitch the completed demo to record labels—all without stepping outside the building. The poem's title is taken from a song by lyricist Gerry Goffin and composer Carole King, a husband-and-wife team who were among the most successful of the many hustling songwriters of that era. This song is best known in the version by The Byrds and was initially recorded for the *Easy Rider* soundtrack.

CLIFFORD BROWN (1930-1956) When word reached the jazz community that Clifford Brown had died in a car accident on the rain-slicked Pennsylvania Turnpike on June 26, 1956 (the accident also claimed pianist Richie Powell and his wife Nancy, who was driving), the community grieved heavily—there were reports of musicians walking off their gigs in grief. And people close to Max Roach, who co-led the Clifford Brown-Max Roach Quintet, said that he never really got over the loss. As a person, Brown was open, engaging and friendly. He totally abstained from illegal drug use, and rarely drank alcohol. Mourners who did not know him personally were grieving the loss of a gifted improviser and a memorable composer. Influenced by his friend, trumpeter Fats Navarro (who also died young, of TB), "Brownie" did not (like some of the bop trumpeters) sacrifice tone and sheer beauty on the altar of technical prowess. He recorded with vocalists Sara Vaughan, Dinah Washington and Helen Merrill, as well as recording a very good album with strings. His band with Roach, which included Sonny Rollins, was a hard bop group already pointing ahead to further developments in jazz. Incredibly, his recording career lasted only four years. He was twenty-five when he died. The title of the poem "I Remember Clifford," is from Benny Golson's composition of the same name, which has become a jazz standard.

Brownie: The Complete Emarcy Recordings of Clifford Brown (UMG)
B rownie Speaks: The Complete Blue Note Recordings

PAUL CHAMBERS (1935–1969). The greatest and most widely recorded bass player of the hard bop era, Chambers is most familiar to casual jazz fans for his 8-year tenure as a Miles Davis sideman—especially on the great album Kind of Blue. Blessed with an acute sense of time and a gorgeous tone, he was a master of the bowed bass solo.

Paul Chambers: Capitol Jazz Vault Series (Capitol)
1st Bassman (Vee-Jay)

SONNY CLARK (1931–1963) A much in demand session pianist, primarily recording in the hard bop idiom, mostly for Blue Note. He was also a distinctive composer whose works were championed by John Zorn. His leadership dates are prized among Japanese jazz collectors and can be often heard in Japan's "*Jazz Kissa*" cafes, where people gather specifically to listen to jazz recordings.

Cool Struttin' (Blue Note)
Sonny's Crib (Blue Note)

BILL CROW (1927–) The amazing Bill Crow has been active as a bass player on the New York City scene since 1952. He has played across a wide range of situations, putting in time from the groups of Gerry Mulligan and Stan Getz, the society band of Peter Duchin, part of the house band at the Playboy Club and being in the pit bands of numerous Broadway shows. He is the author of two books of jazz anecdotes and an autobiography, *From Birdland to Broadway*, all published by Oxford University Press. The photo of Bill Crow crossing Times Square in the early morning after a gig says a lot about the music and the era. Many thanks to Magnum Photo for permission to use this classic image.

TED CURSON (1935–2012) A versatile player, his trumpet work was featured on albums by such advanced players as Cecil Taylor, Archie Shepp and Eric Dolphy. He is best known to listeners for his work with Charles Mingus' adventurous groups of the early '60s sharing the frontline with Dolphy. The photo of Bill Crow crossing Times Square in the early morning after a gig says a lot about the music and the era. Many thanks to Magnum Photo for permission to use this classic image.

Tears for Dolphy (Fontana)
Flip Top (Freedom)

MILES DAVIS (1926-1991) Davis is one of the giants in the history of jazz. As a trumpeter, he was not a technical wizard like contemporaries Lee Morgan or Dizzy Gillespie; rather he had that "sound," indentifiable within a few bars and recognizable to a large segment of even the non-jazz audience. A restless musician, he went through numerous phases, beginning as a founder of the "Cool School" and at the end of his life. collaborating with hip-hoppers. Much has been written about him, but his *Miles, The Autobiography* is a vivid document of an iconoclast who also recorded the best-selling jazz album of all time: *Kind of Blue.*

Complete Prestige Recordings 1951-1956 (Prestige)
Complete Bitches Brew Sessions (CBS)

BOOKER ERVIN (1930–1970) When I interviewed pianist Randy Weston, he remarked that Ervin, who played in his groups, "was on the same level as Coltrane"—a sentiment shared by his coterie of admirers. Emerging from the school of hard playing "Texas tenors", Ervin is best known for his contribution to Charles Mingus groups of the late '50s and early '60s. Although he recorded prolifically as a leader, lack of performing opportunities caused him to relocate to Europe for a period in the mid-'60s.

The Space Book (Prestige)
Booker 'n' Brass (World Pacific)

BILL EVANS (1929-1980) Piano master whose influence can be heard in the styles of most contemporary jazz pianists—those recorded by the German ECM label seem particularly in his thrall. For many classical fans, Evans is the only jazz musician that many pay attention to—the reclusive Glen Gould was even a phone buddy. The poem "Gloria's Step" is derived from a Scott LaFaro composition that remained in Evans' repertoire until his death. The poem itself is based on a conversation I had with the late poet/jazz beau Larry Fagin who reported that a new edition of the classic Village Vanguard sessions, digitalized from the original source tapes, were so crystalline that one could now hear the conversations going on at the tables. Also, at the time of the poem's composition, I had been reading reports in the news of a manatee in the Hudson River. "The manatee was said to have been swum past Manhattan and up the Hudson River, at least several miles north of the Tappan Zee Bridge." (*South Florida Sun Sentinel*, August 21, 2006)

The Complete Vanguard Sessions (Milestone)
A Catalog of Jazz (UMG)

RED GARLAND (1923--1984). Pianist Garland was an essential part of Miles Davis' recordings and working groups during the trumpeter's tenure with Prestige records. Many of the standards that Davis recorded in that period were a result of Garland's encyclopedic knowledge of the Great American Songbook. Critic Ralph J. Gleason noted "Red Garland has the sublime virtue of swing and a solid and deep groove."

Red in Bluesville (Prestige)
All Kinds of Weather (Prestige)

STAN GETZ (1927–1991) To many of his fans, tenor saxophonist Getz was simply known as "The Sound" because of his lush and dreamy tone, heavily influenced by Lester Young. As a teenager he played in numerous big bands, becoming a star with Woody Herman. Launching a solo career, he soon became associated with the West Coast "Cool School" of jazz. When he introduced U.S. audiences to Bossa Nova—the last big craze before the British Invasion landed on our shores—he became a pop star. The fabulist poem, "Wrap Your Troubles in Dreams, " is derived from a sentence in Donald Maggin's essential *Stan Getz: A Life in Jazz* (Morrow, 1996): "After an initial burst of anger, he rapidly became depressed, but found some solace in attending Yom Kippur services with Alpert on October 7." (p.368)

Focus (Verve)
Complete Roost Recordings (Roost)

CHARLIE HADEN (1937–2014) Haden was revered among fans and fellow musicians; it was not only because of his innovative approach to bass playing that allowed him to move between strict accompaniment and direct interaction in group improvisation—it was also his deep political and interpersonal commitments. He had a career-long engagement with Ornette Coleman and spent a significant period working with Keith Jarrett. Of his own groups, the most famous is the Liberation Music Orchestra, which used political and folk songs as a springboard for improvising with orchestrations by Carla Bley. The source for his poem is Ethan Iverson's Do *The Math blog.*

The Ballad of The Fallen (ECM)
In Angel City (Verve)

JOHN LEE HOOKER (1917–2001) Hooker stands as a unique figure in blues music—straddling the line between Delta Blues and the electric sound associated with the blues players who migrated to the big cities of the North. His "boogie" sound had great influence on numerous '60s era rock bands, especially Canned Heat. He may be best known for his appearance in the Blues Brothers movie, recorded live on Chicago's Maxwell Street. My acquisition of *the Hooker 'n' Heat* LP (that is, Hooker collaborating with Canned Heat) led me away from the popular white blues bands of the era into a serious investigation of the sources of the black music continuum.

Don't Turn Me From Your Door (Atlantic)
The Complete '50s Chess Recordings (Chess)

LEE KONITZ (1927–2020). One of the few alto saxophonists of the bop era who developed a distinctive style outside of the enormous shade of Charlie Parker, Konitz began as a disciple of Lennie Tristano and went on to perform in myriad styles ranging from "cool" to free improvisation. Lee Konitz: Conversations on the Improvisers Art (Andy Hamilton, University of Michigan Press, 2007) is one of great books on improvising from the performer's viewpoint.

Inside Hi-Fi (Atlantic)
Motion (Verve)

WARNE MARSH (1927–1987) Sax player Marsh came from an affluent Hollywood family—his father was a prominent cinematographer, and his aunt was actress Mae Marsh. He came to New York City and began a period of study with Lennie Tristano, eventually joining the pianist's working groups. Marsh was the most faithful of Tristano's disciples; his tenor playing was even toned and focused on improvising on long lines that avoid using licks or musical quotes. His repertoire consisted primarily of exploring a small body of jazz standards. Anthony Braxton has long cited Marsh as an influence, as does fellow tenor player Mark Turner.

Warne Marsh (Atlantic)
Apogee (Warner Brothers)

THELONIUS MONK (1917–1982) One of the handful of jazz musicians whose popularity extends far beyond the jazz community. Jean-Paul Sartre dug him, and the highly cerebral Milton Babbbit composed a variation on Monk's famous composition, "Round Midnight." Within the jazz community, only Duke Ellington's works are performed more than Monk's (and Monk only composed about 70 tunes as opposed to Ellington's over 2,000). In addition to his compositions, there is Monk's highly original and immediately identifiable piano style—ultra-percussive, strategically dissonant, angular, and with an uncanny use of silence. Monk was the house pianist at the bop incubator Minton's Playhouse and can be heard on the sessions recorded in 1941 by Kerouac's college buddy Jerry Newman on a portable acetate machine featuring boppers Kenny Clarke and Don Byas. Monk, however, who claimed James P. Johnson, Duke Ellington and church music as influences was an outlier on the bop scene, though Blue Note records promoted him as "The High Priest of Bop"—which probably scared away many potential listeners. It was not until Monk signed to Riverside records in the mid-'50s that he finally emerged as a major figure in jazz—culminating in his unlikely 1964 appearance on the cover of *Time* Magazine. There have been over 75 Monk tribute albums, as well as several jazz units whose repertoire is all Monk all the time. The title of this book derives from a 1944 composition which remained in Monk's repertoire throughout his career. According to Robin D.G. Kelly's excellent *Thelonius Monk: The Life and Times of an American Original*, "Well, You Needn't," the Monk composition by inspired by vocalist Charlie Beamon, who, when told that the new song would be named for him, replied "Well, you needn't".

The Complete Blue Note recordings of Thelonius Monk (Blue Note)
The Complete Riverside Recordings of Thelonius Monk (Riverside/Fantasy)

LEE MORGAN (1938–1972) Morgan began recording in his late teens and soon established himself in the first rank of hard bop trumpeters as a long-standing member of Art Blakey's Jazz Messengers. Most of his leadership dates were for Blue Note and he had a crossover hit with his composition "Sidewinder." His tragic end at the hands of his girlfriend is documented in the film *I Called Him Morgan*.

The Rumproller (Blue Note)
Live At the Lighthouse (Blue Note)

SUNNY MURRAY (1936-2017) Murray was a pioneer free jazz percussionist—abandoning the jazz drummer's traditional role of time keeping, focusing instead on textural playing that responds to the other musicians in the ensemble. The Cecil Taylor album *Nefertiti the Beautiful One Has Come* offered a potent example of Murray's breakthrough. He soon joined Albert Ayler's group and recorded extensively with them, including the breakthrough album *Spiritual Unity*. Murray led his own groups and recoded numerous leadership and sideman dates, mostly in Europe where he settled. The poem title, "A Conductor of Energies," is derived from an essay about him by Amiri Baraka.

Sunny Murray (ESP Disk)
An Even Break (BYG/Actuel)

CHARLIE PARKER (1920-1955) The general musical public's perception of Charlie Parker is rooted in the alto saxophonist's many excesses (drugs, sex, various bad behaviors) amplified by writers like Jack Kerouac. Conversely, serious fans study Parker's solos in various recorded takes and live recordings in the manner that rabbinic scholars study the *Talmud*. Parker's very short career literally changed the direction of jazz, shifting it from ballrooms filled with dancers to clubs filled with listeners. Stanley Crouch's *Kansas City Lightning: The Rise and Times of Charlie* is the best book account of Parker, though it only takes the saxophonist up through his early career. Clint Eastwood's film *Bird* is worth watching—the director is a great jazz fan (as well as a piano player) and took great pains to present Parker's life in an authentic manner.

Jazz at Massey Hall (Fantasy)
The Complete Dial and Savoy Masters

BERNARD PURDIE (1939–) Purdie was the leading New York City session drummer during the '60s and '70s; he was so in demand, according to his ex-producer Bob Porter (one of the characters in this book!), that he was the rare NYC session musician who had an answering service in the days before voice-mail. Best known for his soul sessions (especially Aretha Franklin), he also did a fair amount of jazz work. My fabulist poem about their lunch together is rooted in Purdie's participation in Ayler's ill-fated *New Grass*, a pop-oriented album that deeply alienated both critics and fans, and failed commercially as well. Two good examples of Purdie's legendary and much copied/sampled "Purdie Shuffle" can be found in his performance on Steely Dan's "Babylon Sisters" and "Home At Last."

Soul Drums (Columbia)
Legends of Acid Jazz: Bernard Purdie (Prestige)

SONNY SHARROCK (1940–1994) One of the few guitarists involved in the first burst of the Free Jazz movement, Sharrock come to attention in Pharoah Sanders' groups and achieved wider visibility as a member of Herbie Mann's very popular late-'60s-early-'70s ensemble. His admirers include fellow guitarists Vernon Reid, Thurston Moore and Carlos Santana. The text of "Seize the Rainbow" I derived from a Sharrock interview that appeared in *Motorbooty #5*, 1990

Black Woman (Vortex)
Ask The Ages (Axiom)

ARCHIE SHEPP (1937–). Part of the first wave of "New Thing" jazz artists, the tenor saxophonist initially recorded with pianist Cecil Taylor and soon came to attention of John Coltrane. Shepp was part of the large ensemble that recorded Coltrane's album-length free jazz masterpiece Ascension. At Coltrane's urging, Shepp was signed to his mentor's label, Impulse, and recorded some of the most innovative albums of the early Free Jazz era. Since the mid-70s, his musical palette widened as he has recorded in a myriad of black musical idioms. A forceful critic and polemicist, he taught for 30 years at UMass/Amherst before relocating to Paris. "Archie

Shepp Recalls His First Encounter with Miles Davis" is sourced from an interview published in Jazz Times (2020)

Fire Music (Impulse)
Goin' Home (Steeplechase)

JIMMY SMITH (1928-2005) Yet another gifted jazz musician from the Philadelphia area (he attended the same music school as John Coltrane), Smith virtually created the soul jazz idiom, which tended to be ignored by critics and "serious" fans, but found its core audience at clubs in working-class black neighborhoods. His core albums are those on Blue Note, which featured long tracks and label stars like Art Blakey and Lee Morgan.

The Sermon (Blue Note)
House Party (Blue Note)

LENNIE TRISTANO (1919–1978) A blind pianist who came to prominence in the early bop era, Tristano was admired for his linear approach to improvisation and his complex harmonic sense. He recorded the first examples of free group improvisation in the late '40s. He gradually withdrew from both recording and public performance and devoted his time to teaching—he was the first to teach jazz improvisation in a systematic manner.

CrossCurrents (Capitol)
Lennie Tristano (Atlantic)

BEN WEBSTER (1909-1973). Though not as adventurous or pathbreaking as his contemporaries Lester Young and Coleman Hawkins, tenor saxophonist Webster was admired for breathy, vibrato-rich solos on ballads, and a pugilistic approach to up-tempo numbers. He was a member of Duke Ellington's most significant ensemble, referred to by historians as "The Blanton-Webster Band" (1940–1943). Webster, however, was a major headache among the many headache-inducing band members that Ellington endured, and he eventually departed, spending much of his later career in small units, eventually settling in Copenhagen, where there is a charitable foundation that bears his name.

King of The Tenor (Verve)
Soulmates (Riverside)

PHIL WOODS (1931–2015) Alto saxophonist Woods was a disciple of Charlie Parker who matured into a distinctive and inventive improviser. A Juilliard graduate who also studied with Lennie Tristano, Woods' early career found him playing in the big bands of Quincy Jones, Dizzy Gillespie and Oliver Nelson because of both his impeccable sight-reading skills and his brilliant solos. After a sojourn in Europe, where he experimented with electronics, he returned both to his musical roots and to the USA, becoming a popular concert and festival attraction. The source of the poem “Drifting on a Reed” is an interview conducted by Marc Myers that appeared in his Jazz Wax blog.

Rights of Swing (Candid)
Musique du Bois (Muse)

BILL ZAVATSKY (1943–) Zavatsky is an American poet, a translator from the French, and an able jazz pianist. He was a close friend of Bill Evans in that pianist’s last years. Zavatsky’s poem “Elegy: For Bill Evans (1929-1980)” was included on the back cover of the posthumous Evans LP *You Must Believe In Spring.* Richard Twardzik (as cited in the poem “Chatting With Zavatsky”) was a brilliant, advanced pianist who as leader made a single 10-inch LP with Russ Freeman, *Trio* (Pacific Jazz) and died of a heroin overdose while on tour with Chet Baker at age 24. Twardzik’s name is used a sort of password to separate the serious jazz fan from the dilettante.

*

NOTES ON THE POEMS

Some of these poems reflect, and frequently quote from, sources that led me to their creation. Others are purely found poems, and indicated as such.

All sourcing is noted; other quotes are my own invention.

The Sonny Rollins quote is from the forthcoming Notebooks of Sonny Rollins, quoted in the *New York Times* Book Review.

Names of songs, in poem titles and text, are in quotes.

Names of albums, in poem titles and text, are in italics.

I regret that I was unable to provide even brief biographies of every musician I have mentioned in this book. That would have required hundreds of pages. I can only say here that I have huge gratitude and respect for all of the musicians who gave themselves to Jazz, and who gave Jazz to us.

*

A GUIDE FOR THE MUSICALLY PERPLEXED

I make no claims to being a jazz historian—I prefer the term "digger," as in the classic "jive" formulation, "Can you dig it?" (my old boss Bob Porter tried to start up a jazz magazine called The Digger, to which I actually submitted a review of an album by Bob's particular bête noire, Gato Barbieri). But I can provide brief definitions of some of the major schools of jazz—definitions that are a little approximate, given the wide range of opinions that define these musical paths.

Please note that most of these schools were the creations of fans, critics and the promotion departments of record labels. Many bop musicians made soul jazz albums. Cool jazz players often recorded tunes associated with bop and hard bop. Fusion players like Chick Corea and Herbie Hancock continued to record and perform acoustic jazz. Many of the early Free Jazz performers, like Archie Shepp and Pharoah Sanders, played much more conventional music in their later years. Jazz being a commercially marginal music, many musicians had to make choices driven by economics rather than aesthetics.

CLASSIC JAZZ, also called Traditional Jazz, Dixieland and Hot Jazz. As with most popular music forms, there is no "inventor" of jazz—it is safer to say that the music was developed by African-American musicians in the multi-cultural charivari that is New Orleans. This early jazz includes elements of ragtime, marching band music and perhaps touches of Sicilian and French music. The two great geniuses of this classic style are Jelly Roll Morton, a vivid composer and perhaps the first to arrange the music for an ensemble; and Louis Armsrong, whose amazing solos are still studied, and whose Hot Five & Seven ensembles focus the music towards individual improvising—there is in fact some evidence to suggest that it was Armstrong himself who first created the art and the practice of improvisation.

Gunther Schuller's *Early Jazz: Its Roots and Classical Development* (Oxford University Press, revised edition 1986) is a classic study of this music.

SWING MUSIC. This genre's beginnings go back to the mid-1920s with Don Redmond's arrangements for Fletcher Henderson's dance band; these featured faster tempos in 4/4 time and solos backed by arranged accompaniments. Duke Ellington credited Henderson as a major influence on his newly established orchestra. The combination of radio broadcasts and the flush economy of the '20s spread the music across the country.

Many place the start of the so-called "Swing Era" at Benny Goodman's 1935 appearance at the Palomar Ballroom. During this period (1935-1946), jazz became popular music, especially among a young white audience. And, as befitting such a major music trend, swing created a culture around it—real fans were called "Hep-cats," white youth began speaking the language of "jive," "Jitterbuggers" began appearing in the ballroom and the "real gone" Hepcats wore Zoot Suits; the extravagances of such attire got it banned during WW2 as wasteful.

The two great bands of the period were Count Basie's Orchestra, a "hot" swing band with many great soloists, the most significant of whom was Lester Young on tenor sax; and Basie's friendly rival, Duke Ellington. Ellington's group was a singular musical organization that married the marvelous compositions of Ellington and his writing partner Billy Strayhorn to an orchestra of impeccable and well-paid musicians. They often stayed with Ellington for decades. The orchestra traveled across the country in a private Pullman train, mainly to avoid the indignities that could be suffered by black musicians trying to find food and accommodations in a segregated America. During this period, jazz was the dance music for its (particularly young) fans.

The combination of the rise of the solo singer (set off by Frank Sinatra's emergence), the travel restrictions of WW2, and recording bans instigated by the musician unions, marked the end of an era. The pathbreaking Louis Jordan with his "Tympany Five" demonstrated that an ensemble much smaller than the swing bands could profitably perform, tour, and become very popular. Soon the imagination of the young was captured by energetic and sometimes anarchic jump music, and the emergence of sophisticated Rhythm and Blues (R 'n' B).

Once again, Gunther Schuller comes to the rescue for those interested in a deeper dive: *The Swing Era: The Development of Jazz 1930-1945* (Oxford University Press, 1991).

BEBOP. This jazz idiom extended many of the advances developed by swing music. However, bebop (and there are a number of origin stories for that term), moves jazz from a music for dancing to a quasi-art music. As opposed to the Swing big band, the classic bop group was like many R'n'B bands, smaller, usually a quintet—rhythm section with saxophone and trumpet up front. The tone scientists who gave birth to the music were alto sax player Charlie Parker—widely acknowledged as the greatest of jazz innovators—trumpeter Dizzy Gillespie, drummer Kenny Clarke and pianist Bud Powell. They introduced complex chord changes, advanced harmonics and a varied and dynamic rhythm sense, as bop drummers followed Kenny Clarke's lead in moving beyond traditional timekeeping.

In its time, Bop was jazz's version of Punk Rock—the bands of Stan Kenton and Woody Herman were more popular, there was a simultaneous revival of traditional jazz that was so popular that even William Carlos Williams went to hear (and wrote a poem about) Bunk Johnson, a long-forgotten trumpeter discovered by fans who raised money for dentures that allowed him to perform again. In the jazz world of today, bop is the standard and basis of study for the many college jazz programs around the world.

Two books worth reading on bop are Scott DeVaux's *The Birth Of Bop* (University of California Press , 1999), and poet Lewis McAdams' *Birth of the Cool: Beat, BeBop and the American AvantGarde* (Free Press, 2001), which provides a social history of the music and the community which embraced it.

HARD BOP — A variant of bebop, a style influenced by gospel music and the rising rhythm and blues scene of the early 50s (with the jazz-infused music of Ray Charles as a major influence). Art Blakey's 1957 album *Hard Bop* gave a name to this genre. Blakey's working group, The Jazz Messengers (originally co-founded with pianist Horace Silver), is the most realized of all the hard bop units—members were required to compose for the band; all of Blakey's groups were disciplined and well-rehearsed. Many labels recorded hard bop, but it was those for Blue Note Records that stand out. Blue Note paid for a pre-recording rehearsal session and would hold back sessions they felt inferior The emergence of the LP as the primary recording medium allowed for longer track times and more relaxed, even danceable, tempos. Hard Bop had a revival during the early ascendancy of Wynton Marsalis and the "Young Lions" movement and, even today, most young jazz musicians could be woken out of a deep sleep and be immediately ready to play the compositions of Benny Golson, Horace Silver and Hank Mobley without recourse to sheet music.

David H.Rosenthal's *Hard Bop and Black Music 1955-1965* (OUP) is a good resource for those looking to dive deeper into this music.

SOUL JAZZ is often seen as a variant of hard bop, with the music leaning harder on rhythm and blues influences and with an effort towards appealing to a black urban audience. Foundational figures are tenor saxophonists Stanley Turrentine and Eddie "Lockjaw" Davis, and the very popular Cannoball Adderly Quintet. The most common configuration of the Soul Jazz combo featured a Hammond B-3 organ, which not only evoked the sound of the black church but was the loudest instrument on a bandstand before the emergence of the solid body rock guitar. One of the most successful and longstanding soul units was that of tenor saxophonist Houston Person, featuring the great vocalist, Etta Jones. Houston was a frequent visitor to Jazz Etc. as my boss Bob Porter produced many of his albums. Soul Jazz was mostly ignored by critics and "serious" fans, finding its audiences rather in black neighborhood clubs. Porter in his study *Soul Jazz: Jazz in the Black Community 1945-1975* cites the rise of disco as causing its demise—many clubs replaced live music with DJs and sound systems. Soul Jazz enjoyed a revival and a higher level of respect with the rise of Hip-Hop. "Crate-digging" DJs began sampling drum breaks, bass lines and melodies from Soul Jazz albums often found in used record shops, thrift stores or in the collection of somebody's grandparents. In some quarters it was rebranded as "Acid Jazz"; labels like Blue Note and Prestige began issuing collections aimed at the samplers. Against the usual flow of things, those whose music was sampled—or more often, the deceased musician's family—were compensated, often receiving checks larger than anything they'd earned when the music was recoded.

COOL JAZZ was a very popular genre of the '50s, often scorned by the era's bop and hard bop fans, and by many jazz critics. It's closely identified with Miles Davis' 1957 LP album *Birth of the Cool* (which incorporated his1949 and 1950 78s). Its also commonly called West Coast Jazz as most of its major performers were based in Los Angeles. The music is typified by relaxed tempos and a lighter tone, influenced by both saxophonist Lester Young and elements of classical music. To the wider music public, the musician most identified with Cool/West Coast Jazz was Chet Baker. His gentle tenor voice, a trumpet style owing much to Miles Davis, and his good looks all combined to make him something of a pop star before heroin upended his career. However, the music is far more expansive than its critics will allow. I'd point readers to drummer Shelly Manne's *At the Black Hawk*, a five-volume set of LPs, as an example of West Coast Jazz at its best. The label that best documented West Coast players was Contemporary Records, sort of a California cousin to Blue Note in their attention to sound, album design and focus on unfettered straight-ahead playing. The label even recorded the first two Ornette Coleman albums and an early Cecil Taylor record.

Ted Gioia's *West Coast Jazz: Modern Jazz in California 1945–1960* (Oxford University Press), is the standard history of the music.

POST BOP is a somewhat vague term, but it describes a style of jazz that developed from the Miles Davis Quintet of the mid-'60s, which featured Wayne Shorter, Herbie Hancock, Ron Carter and Tony Williams. In general, Post Bop departs from the conventions of hard bop, but stops short of the musical rule-breaking of the Jazz avant-garde that was concurrent with the style. Blue Note documented this style through albums by artists such as Shorter, Hancock, Andrew Hill and Bobby Hutcherson; outside of Hancock's albums, these discs sold poorly at their release but are foundational for much of the current jazz one hears.

Jeremy Yudkin's *Miles Davis, Miles Smiles and the Invention of Post Bop (Indiana University Press)* is a thoughtful study of a music that I am always returning to as a listener.

FREE JAZZ derives its name from the title of Ornette Coleman's most ambitious album for Atlantic, *Free Jazz: A Collective Improvisation*, which featured a continuous performance by a "double quartet." Although musicians through the '50s made attempts at pushing jazz past chordal improvisation, it was Coleman's music—simultaneously looking back at jazz's origins and towards its future—which created a movement that has persisted worldwide, despite a narrow appeal and the Bob Porters of the world shouting "turn that off". The catalog of ESP-Disk documented the first players to follow Coleman's path and Impulse records documented the explorations of John Coltrane and his associates.

John Litweiler's *The Freedom Principle: Jazz After 1958* and *Ornette Coleman: A Harmelodic Life* (both *Da Cap Books)* are two excellent books on the early years of the free jazz movement.

FUSION. I'll close out these mini-surveys with the music that originally pulled me into the jazz vortex. Originally called "jazz-rock," Fusion was first associated with performers like Gary Burton, Larry Coryell and Steve Marcus. Miles Davis' *Bitches Brew* conferred some legitimacy on the widening of the jazz spectrum to include electric instruments and rock rhythms, and to engender an atmosphere closer to the hippies than to the hipsters. It was was John McLaughlin's Mahavishnu Orchestra that broke fusion to the rock audience. Under the management of Nat Weiss, the group played hundreds of shows sharing the bill with rock bands of many stripes. Mahavishnu was VERY loud: McLaughlin made most rock guitarists seem like amateurs; soon enough the word spread about this band, its leader dressed in white and sporting a crew cut (something to do with a guru). Most of the first wave of fusion groups was made up of former Miles Davis sidemen—Herbie Hancock's Headhunters, Chick Corea's Return to Forever and Weather Report. Fusion albums were recorded like rock albums, utilizing the potential of 18-track mixers to create a layered and fuller sound that appealed to rock-attuned ears. Perhaps the most archetypal fusion tune is Weather Report's "Birdland", written by the group's keyboard player Joe Zawinul, which is a tribute to the temple of bebop—Birdland, the jazz club on 52nd Street. The rise of Fusion was a source of agony to the older jazz community, as many of the performers were very accomplished acoustic players with impeccable credentials. In the early '80s, trumpeter and composer Wynton Marsalis revived an interest in acoustic jazz, which was often seen as a response and a corrective to fusion. Fusion has never quite gone away, though it has evolved into a self-contained genre with less obvious jazz influences.

Kevin Fellezs; *Birds of Fire: Jazz, Rock, Funk, and The Creation of* Fusion (Duke University Press) is an academic study for anyone interested in serious reading about this music.